Managing by the
Law of the Sphere

How to Organize a Business
for Maximum Profitability

MANAGING BY THE
LAW OF THE SPHERE

HOW TO ORGANIZE A BUSINESS
FOR MAXIMUM PROFITABILITY

DAVID Y. BLUM

Rutledge Books, Inc.      Danbury, CT

Rutledge Books, Inc.
107 Mill Plain Road, Danbury, CT 06811
1-800-278-8533
www.rutledgebooks.com
info@rutledgebooks.com

Manufactured in the United States of America

Cataloging in Publication Data
Blum, David Y.
    Managing by the law of the sphere
        ISBN: 1-58244-014-X
            1. Business -- Handbooks, manuals, etc.
            2. Strategic planning.
658 / .022

Dedication

This book is dedicated
to my son Pierre, Editor *par excellence*.

Contents

Introduction

Having started and operated my own successful company, I thought I should share my knowledge about how to properly organize a company and to have fun making profit in the process. Nothing contributes more to the stress level of a company leader than a red balance sheet. Losing money is no fun.

There are literally hundreds of business how to or how to manage books around so why write another one? My answer is, look at the authors. Most of them are consultants who have never run a successful business but who are clever at inventing new slogans. You have to wade through 200 or more pages propagating: Reengineering management, one must have vision; you must call your employees associates; have quality circles; have a mission; shared values; and so on. You probably still don't know how to motivate and reward your employees, how to organize your computer system, how to spot wasteful fads, how to communicate with customers, how to staff non-productive departments, and other very down to earth problems.

The proposed Law of the Sphere provides a mathematical

tool to help predict the increase in the number of supportive personnel (overhead) when companies grow. This, in turn, could serve as a guide on how to structure a company in order to maintain profitability.

All anecdotal information and tabulated data are based on facts with the sole exception of the probably classified data shown on page 38 and 39. Unless indicated otherwise, I did not state company names in order to avoid unnecessary embarrassment.

The recommendations laid down in this book may be unconventional, and perhaps controversial, but have proven to be highly successful and, hopefully, will guide you to success in starting or running a company, a division, or department.

I hope some budding entrepreneur or seasoned executives will read this book and benefit from it. If, consequently, I can contribute to the economic well being of my country, then that shall be my reward.

The casual reader of this book may infer that I dislike computers. This is far from the truth. There are thousands of functions where computers are literally indispensable in our complex world.

What I do object to and try to highlight is the widespread misuse or misapplication of computers and computer software. That is what contributes to draining company profits and what decreases operating efficiencies.

Chapter 1

INCENTIVES AND DISINCENTIVES

Money outweighs coercion when
it comes to work incentives

As Scott Adams* (a.k.a. Dilbert) rightfully pointed out, "Nobody likes to work, otherwise people would pay their employers for the privilege."

What we need are incentives to cause otherwise healthy and smart people to get off their couches or leave the golf courses to go to a factory or office. Compensation, of course, is a powerful incentive. We all require money to pay for the necessities of life such as food, clothing, rent, or even alimony payments. But salary or wages alone are not often enough to stimulate a cohesive workforce, unless the pay is related directly to a measurable performance such as payment for the number of widgets produced in an hour or a

---

* Scott Adams, "The Dilbert Principle," (Harper Collins, 1996).

commission on a sale. Unfortunately, the output of the over-whelming majority of the labor force cannot be directly measured so it behooves management to provide incentives to encourage labor to work *voluntarily* towards a common goal, such as a company's profits.

In order for incentives to be effective, they must be (a) measurable, (b) guaranteed, (c) fair, (d) time limited, and (e) stimulate group performance. Incentive plans that do not meet these requirements are a waste of money, time, and effort. Governments try to stimulate employee group performance in state-run enterprises by appealing to ideology, patriotism, and by telling employees they are working for their own company (since the government is run by the people and the factory is run by the government; hence, the factory is owned by the people!). None of this works as the politicians of the former Soviet Union found out to their chagrin.

After starting my own company, I thought an incentive plan would help motivate my employees. Besides, I truly wanted my employees to feel that they were a part of the enterprise. While I maintained a separate bonus plan for key managers, I devised a very simple plan to distribute a portion of the company's profits to all other employees. Since the company was on a fiscal calendar year, we would pay about 1/2 of the estimated bonus before Christmas and the final balance (after the books were audited) around the middle of March. The percentage was based on half of the net operating profit before interest and tax and usually amounted to between 9.5 and 12.8% of an employee's yearly wages or salary.

Having two payouts is psychologically important. Like any pleasurable experience in life, the biggest and longest lasting effect lies in *expecting* the benefits. We derive as much, if not more, pleasure *looking forward* to taking a vacation than actually experiencing the trip itself, which may turn out to be disappointing depending upon the circumstances. This is even more true when paying a bonus. The pleasure of expecting the money increases in inverse proportion to the waiting period for the money. Once the money is deposited, the bonus becomes a past event and its value to the employee quickly diminishes. Therefore, having two pay periods increases the stimulus. Any pay-out period exceeding one year becomes too long for proper stimulation. The brain cannot comprehend time periods of several years.

It is also important to keep the employees informed periodically about the estimated profits of the company. This will keep up the reward expectancy. As for fairness, it goes without saying that management should never renege on awarding bonuses, nor change the terms *during* a business year. One of the most important, beneficial effects of a group incentive is to stimulate the performance of the whole company. Here is where a good profit sharing plan shines. Every employee knows without prompting (sometimes by hideous cartoon-type posters put up by management) that company profits depend not only on his or her own performance, but also on the performance of their fellow workers. I have had employees go to their supervisors to complain about certain individuals who *were not performing well* and recommended they be reprimanded! It also prompts other company beneficial actions such as employees notifying supervisors of low inventory on certain key parts, volunteering overtime in order to ship an emergency order to a customer, and so on. What is most important is that this striving for effectiveness as an organization extends beyond the individual's department. It was not uncommon for an individual to volunteer to help out in another department busier than his own. All traits absent in companies having only individual performance-based bonuses, or none at all!

As an example, I know of a company that was sold to a much larger organization (with the group bonus plan still intact), the new president, doing what was customary in his former place of work, called an *all employees* group meeting which consisted of a pep talk outlining the future of the company in such terms as *S.I.P., best cost producer, order fulfillment, customer satisfaction actions, product differentiation, enterprise system,* and other terminology and acronyms which were new and incomprehensible to the bewildered employees who were accustomed to being addressed in plain English by the former CEO. The rest of the day was spent watching safety-related videos made by some *not-for-profit* department of the parent corporation (after purchasing a theater size video screen and matching high-power amplifying system) to teach how not to step in front of a forklift or how to recognize the color code of dangerous chemical containers (never used in this company).

The next day I talked with one of the employees who looked gloomy. She responded to my query on how the meeting went by saying: "Well, it was okay, but we lost a full day of production. I wonder how it will affect our profit sharing bonus?"

As I stated before, individual performance bonuses are okay, but only for managers of key departments. Even here, discretion and strategic planning is of importance. For example, it is very tempting and common to give the sales manager a bonus tied to the order volume of a company. This is a serious error, since it will result in an instant increase in the discount given to customers with a resultant decrease in the profit level of the company. The sales manager knows quite well that if you extend the discount level over that of your competitors', you book more orders; hence, a bigger bonus.

I overcame this problem by making the sales bonus tied into the profit figures. For example, if bookings went up five percent over the prior year, and the profit was 20%, then his total bonus was 5 x (20/10) = 10%. However, if bookings went up 20% over the target set at the beginning of the year (and agreed upon by the manager), and the profit was only 2%, then his bonus was reduced to only 20 x (2/10) = 4%! This is a powerful incentive not to decrease prices unnecessarily.

A similar bonus plan can be devised for a production manager. Here the key next to profit could be *ship-on-time*. For instance, a bonus plan could look like this: Bonus = % profit x (% ship-on-time^2/10,000). If profit is 12% and ship-on-time is 78%, then the bonus is 12 x (78^2/10,000) = 7.3%. If ship-on-time is 98% (as it should be!), then the bonus is 11.5%. A powerful incentive to service the customer.

5

In his book, Reengineering Management,* James Champy quoted Ira Walters of AT&T Universal Card Services: "The essence of our compensation program is divided into two components. One, is our base pay, which is fairly typical. Then we have a rather rich variable pay program which is contingent on business outcomes thus supporting a company-wide incentive plan." A similar plan by Hannaford Bros. Company was also quoted as being based on overall company budget achievement. In this case, the yearly bonus averaged about 9%. No wonders both of these companies are successful.

Another powerful group incentive is to grant your employees an option to buy stock in your company (assuming it is a *listed* corporation). This is not as effective as a cash bonus (which is a more short-term based payout) tied to profit because stock prices rise and fall with the general stock market trends and not necessarily with each profit announcement by your company. Nevertheless, a stock bonus, that is perhaps subsidized by your management, could serve as a powerful stimulus for company loyalty and group cohesion, especially if it is offered in addition to a traditional year-end cash bonus.

Regardless of the bonus, I made it a point to remind my managers several times during the year that *the company is in business to make money (profit), NOT to manufacture and sell widgets.*

---

* James Champy, Reengineering Management, (London, United Kingdom: Harper Collins, 1995)

While this message may seem hostile to the needs of customers, it really is not. Only a healthy and profitable company is of any use to a customer. This really touches on the heart of the private enterprise system and is what ultimately distinguishes us from socialistic economies. It is therefore paramount for a company president to remind managers of this simple message.

As I mentioned before, putting a whole group on individual performance bonuses will kill the cohesiveness and teamwork of the organization and, therefore, is counter-productive. Other disincentives are perpetuating the purpose of a department whose function, while necessary, is basically profit reducing. Departments dealing with environmental issues come to mind. How can you motivate a manager of such a department to do his best to solve a particular plant clean-up problem and to deal effectively with the involved government agency? The manager knows quite well that with the resolution of this problem, his job may be terminated. The incentive is to *drag* the problem out. To help solve this problem, make this position a temporary transfer from another (profit contributing) department. I am sure this person would be itching to get back to his old job as soon as possible.

A prime example of this type of *absolute* disincentive can be found in the Federal Government. Take the National Cancer Institute, for example. The purpose of the institute is to search for a cure for cancer. Why then does it seem this institute does hardly anything more than design posters to encourage us to stop smoking? The answer should be obvious. Once there is a cure, then there is no more need for this institute. This is the ultimate disincentive.

Picture yourself as the head of the National Cancer Institute with over 5,000 employees, a *zillion* dollar budget*, etc. Suddenly a young scientist enters your office and excitedly proclaims, "Sir, I found a cure for cancer!" You would be sorely tempted to shoot the fellow on the spot.

Here is a summary of incentives and disincentives:

GOOD	BAD
Group incentives (profit sharing)	No incentive
Managerial performance tied to profit and performance.	Individual incentives
Make non-profit contributing jobs distasteful.	Managerial incentives tied to functional performances only.
Make every employee feel he or she is part of a family.	Make non-profitable jobs a career position.

---

* During 1994, the U.S. Government spent $15,900 million on medical research (Source: Statistical Abstract of the United States (Government Printing Office, 1996)

Chapter 2

ENTROPY AND OTHER HEADY STUFF

*A person avoiding work is but following
his or her instinct to conserve energy.*

In order to explain some basic human behavior such as spending money rather than earning it, sitting in committee meetings rather than doing actual work, or enjoying skiing downhill but loathe to walk up the hill, we have to consult the laws of nature, or more precisely, the laws of thermodynamics.

Thermodynamics, which to most is an obscure scientific term, governs our daily lives whether we realize it or not. Like other scientific disciplines, it is governed by fundamental laws: Law number one basically states, *no energy is ever lost*. Law number two states that *energy always degrades to a lower state*, which means it becomes less usable.

While the first law of thermodynamics gives false hopes of never-ending energy sources, thus encouraging unlimited use of available energy (or tax dollars as the economic equivalent), it is the second law's effect we feel. It manifests itself in such things as the continuing decrease in the average American's standard of living since about 1980.*

In scientific terms, when energy *decays* to a lower level, its *entropy* changes, i.e., there are fewer degrees per BTU (degrees per calorie) than before. A similar example in economic terms is inflation. Here the change in entropy is equivalent to less bread for a dollar. We obey this fundamental law at a very young age. Babies enjoy dropping their toys to the floor (expending energy to a lower level from crib to floor), while parents pick up the toy (this increases the available energy by bringing the toy up from the floor). We all recall the expression of satisfaction on the baby's face followed by the frown of the parent. Obviously, the baby is having much more fun.

While steam is the classic carrier of energy in a process plant and loses pressure after passing through a steam engine, thereby *losing available energy* (entropy changes per the second law), so does the value of money if more is spent than available through the production of goods. Note, I only said through goods not services. While only a good fire under a steam boiler can restore the original steam pressure (thus restoring the original entropy), basically only productive

---

* Statistical Abstract of the United States, Bureau of Census (median income of families, wife not in paid labor force, in constant 1994 dollars)

activities in areas such as farming, mining, and manufacturing can restore the value of money, i.e., increase its available energy (entropy) level.

It should be realized that like steam, money is essentially a carrier of energy for our economic system. It would not be far-fetched to peg the value of the dollar on a given number of calories instead of to the weight of gold as has been done before. A number of dollars per barrel of oil could be the measure of international currency, for example.

To make the concept of entropy more understandable, let's consider an example. You are faced with a rock located on top of a hill and one below. To roll the rock down takes very little effort. What we are doing is reducing the available energy (height of the hill times the weight of the rock) to a lower level. On the other hand, lugging the rock uphill is a lot of work and it takes toil and sweat.

This example illustrates how easy it is to expend energy, i.e., spend money rather than make it. In political terms, it takes hardly any effort for a Congressman to vote for a measure that increases expenditure than to vote for a measure that reduces spending. Subconsciously he abides by the second law of thermodynamics. We experience the same in our personal lives. How easy it is to spend a dollar and how hard it becomes to earn it!

With few exceptions, all services performed reduce the available energy of our monetary system. It is, therefore, not possible, as many fashionable book authors have predicted in the 1980's, that the entire United States would convert from a primarily industry-based economy to that of a ser-vice-based economy where we all sit at home and work on computers. The result would be a rapid decrease in value of our money *since an increase in available energy* (increase in monetary value) due to manufacturing, will no longer occur.

Most politicians have a legal background and their exposure to science, let alone thermodynamics, is limited. How else can one explain their decision to build windmills, which during their lifetime of perhaps 20 years, produce signifi-cantly less power than is consumed in the process of melting the steel, copper, and in the machining of parts, in order to produce these windmills. This exercise in futility under the noble name of using *free energy*, i.e., the wind, is only possi-ble by masking the basic economic facts with tax-payer money, i.e., cover the production energy deficit with mone-tary energy (Government grants and tax credits)*. If wind power were really cheap as claimed, you would have seen electric companies exploiting this source years ago! It should also be noted that the government forces generators of con-ventional electricity to buy the electric output of so-called *renewable energy sources* at a cost per kW hour substantially above the cost using their own conventional power plants. Guess who pays for the difference...the consumer. This again is a classic example of the second law of thermodynamics in action! Available energy (national wealth) is reduced to a lower usable level (uneconomical windmills!).

---

* DER SPIEGEL, Vol. 32, (Augstein verlag: Germany, 1990), p. 91.

It may not be a bad idea to give each politician a crash course in the economics of energy. Our country would certainly be better off.

In terms of management policy, consider all administrative or supportive functions as *changing the energy* (of your company) to a lower level. Money (like energy) is spent in the form of salaries, while no profit (excess energy) is generated. Effective personnel involved directly in the production of goods does increase energy, and, therefore, does generate profit (it increases the available energy in the form of monetary value).

Chapter 3

MEETINGS, OR MANAGING BY COMMITTEE

Committee decisions evolve generally around the arguments of the participant who has the maximum stamina and are not necessarily based on the merits of the case.

Domestic Meetings

We seem to be unable to conduct any business at all without having a meeting. This could range from a casual encounter at the water cooler to a friendly business lunch. The latter was my favorite since it combined the necessary with the pleasant. Another advantage of the business lunch is that it establishes a tight time frame for the discussion. Finally, it puts the participants more at ease (who wants to argue on a full stomach?).

In the business world, there are two basic types of meetings:

1. The meeting to inform or instruct. This could be a group of students getting trained, salesmen being told of the merits of a new gadget to be manufactured, a traveling salesman explaining his wares, or the CEO telling his employees that their company has been profitable, to name a few examples.

2. To resolve issues, gain consensus, and make group decisions. This could involve something quite harmless such as deciding on the color of the walls of the executive washroom or something more relevant such as the amount of alcohol added to a mouthwash product. Activities of standards writing committees or board of directors revolve around such meetings.

This second type of meeting has the biggest impact on how companies are run and, more important, on the bottom line. As mentioned before, in order for CEOs to advance through the company hierarchy from relatively obscure positions, they have to rely more and more on the consensus formed in meetings by their department heads who, quite often, rely in turn on a consensus level input from their own subordinates. (This can lead to an absurd case, where the originator of a top-level company policy directive was a lowly mail clerk who somehow missed his calling!)

Since group consensus is never created spontaneously, it takes many meetings for a decision to be made. This then means that the two extreme polarity issues (one that may be truly innovative but daring and the other impractical or absurd) are whittled down to something everybody, or at least most of the members, feel comfortable about. At about the fifth meeting, all but the most persistent advocate of a given issue give up (if for no other reason than sheer boredom) and finally everybody nods his or her head approvingly. Voila! Consensus is achieved.

We all know the adage; "A camel is a race horse designed by committee"...not really a laughing matter. I have known many companies where it is unheard of to have a product developed by responsible individual engineers. The unavoidable consequence of such group design is at best a very mediocre product. One of the more sinister consequences of managing by committee is the subsequent total lack of individual responsibility for a bad policy decision! A committee is a faceless entity; hence, it becomes a comfort factor.

There are, of course, projects that are too big or too multidisciplined to handle or to understand by a single engineer or scientist. However, clear responsibility can be assigned to individual components or portions of the project.

Meetings have evolved into their own culture. There are meetings to plan meetings, meetings to discuss meetings, and don't forget meetings to establish rules for holding meetings. Here are a few names (just add the word *committee*) that most of us are already familiar with: budget, finance, marketing, cost reduction, loss prevention, compensation, safety, environmental, materials, procurement, security, technical steering, standards coordination, computer system, grievance, advisory, management, director, and my favorite...the joint safety, security, and loss prevention committee!

As you can see from the above sampling, there is no single business activity that is immune from our diligent meeting attendees. If we probe deeper, we find that there is the dry-run or try-out meeting, especially prevalent when preparing for budget meetings to insure, among other things, the correct order of overhead slides and that everybody conforms to the party line and nothing embarrassing will ever be said.

To define meetings for the purpose of this discussion, I have in mind not the chance encounter of two employees at the water cooler nor the habitual meeting of elderly and retired gentlemen at the park bench, but the organized get-together of colleagues at a defined location (conference room 435C), a given time (8:30 am), and a fixed agenda.

The typical day of a middle level manager may start with a 7:00 a.m. breakfast meeting with an out-of-town visitor, followed by the weekly *operations* meetings from 8:00 am to typically 11:00 am. At this time he checks his e-mail messages that inform him of meeting schedules for the coming month and specifies his expected contributions. While reviewing his notes, checking his voice mail, and munching on his sandwich for lunch, he is interrupted to be told that the scheduled marketing meeting has been rescheduled from 2:00 p.m. to 1:30 p.m. This leaves him barely enough time to collect and sort his overhead slides before dashing again to this next meeting.

The theme here is not so much what the next product should be in order to help improve the company's sagging bottom line, but how to structure the presentation using the latest (and thanks to highly paid consultants) pyramid schema of added value. This meeting finally comes to an end at 4:00 p.m. after a very lively debate over the question of whether to use two or three parallel overhead projectors at the upcoming top management presentation (three is the consensus, which poses an intriguing question...which one of the three projected texts should be read aloud?).

Going back to his office, he realizes that he is late for his 4:00 p.m. appointment with his out-of-state visitor who, sure enough, sits patiently before his desk. Apologizing and trying frantically to remember the reason for this visit, the embarrassment is overcome by starting a discussion about the latest winning streak of the local professional baseball team. This, if nothing else, will soon establish the needed camaraderie and spirit of *team work* between our hero and the out-of-towner. When the visitor finally leaves at 5:10 p.m., it is time to prepare for the next day, that is, the next day's meetings.

From outward appearances, this has been a very busy day. But you and I may have the nagging question at the back of our minds: What really was accomplished in tangible results? How were sales increased? How was the bottom line (profit) improved? If it was, probably in some obscure way, it certainly was not measurable and probably out of proportion to the salary paid to our hero (which assumption he certainly will hotly deny).

Unfortunately, the above scenario is no exaggeration, but a daily ritual in our corporate structure. As a quite undesirable by-product (from a social to a health problem point of view), this *meeting mania* has spawned a middle management habit of working an excessive amount of overtime and weekend work. How else can you do the other *productive* assignments you are committed to doing (and, if nothing else, write your presentation paper for the next meeting). It is common for middle management employees to work 55 to 60 hours a week, not counting travel time.

Just to show to what extent meetings can go, consider the following true story told to me by a very reliable but understandably unnamed source. A corporate budget review was scheduled for November 1. This started frantic staff work in July to prepare the necessary statistical and backup data. About four weeks later, all department managers were requested to incorporate the proposed budget figures into their respective department budgets with a detailed breakdown on the effects of various line items in the budget not only in the coming year but also on the *next five year plan*.

The end of August saw the first of five typically 1-1/2 day *rehearsal* meetings attended by twenty six participants, each having an average of 56 overhead slides. All were neatly tacked along the wall of the oversized conference room for public review and comments by the *team*. Anything not conforming to the *Leitmotiv* or graphs not presented in the shape of a pyramid were rejected.

On October 15, after the last rehearsal, which, incidentally, always included reading all the fine text of each slide aloud, everything fell into place. Expected questions from the corporate CEO were posed and acceptable answers were rehearsed by everyone (you never knew *whom* he might ask!). The division president sighed with relief: "We are ready!"

Then a bombshell burst...the budget meeting was postponed to January 3rd. This caused a frantic redirection of effort since, after all, there were now two more operating months to consider. Luckily, the bulk of the presentations could be salvaged; therefore, it was only necessary to hold four additional rehearsals before the big day.

Total *rehearsal* costs alone for the man-hours of the meeting attendees: 2800. This translates into about $140,000 in salaries to which you should add at least $100,000 in staff work and travel expenses.

Of course, one should not overlook the very positive human aspects of meetings. Psychologically, meetings satisfy our *herd* instinct, i.e., the need to belong and interact with a group of our peers. This need becomes more and more important since increasing numbers of office employees are penned up in office cubicles or spend lonely hours in front of computer screens without any face-to-face human interaction. This is a need for *belonging* that has to be satisfied in a healthy office environment.

It is a worthy challenge for a good manager to provide effective ways for employees to *come together* and to satisfy this part of their emotional want while avoiding repeatedly scheduled, time-wasting, and inefficient meeting rituals.

International Meetings

So far, I have discussed planned internal or domestic meetings, but there are others on the international level that may well have an impact on our financial well being. For example, international standards meetings have the lofty ideal of making things worldwide interchangeable. This is generally true only for relatively new technologies that have not seen a billion dollars worth of installed base of nationally differently designed gadgets such as the wall outlet for electrical appliances, which to every world traveler's chagrin is different in practically every country.

The unfortunate result of adopting one set of dimensions over that of another country is the very high cost of retooling for the *loser* country.

Here is an example: In 1971 when the International Standards Organization (ISO) tried to standardize the installed length of industrial valves, they initially rejected the U.S. proposal for U.S. dimensions on the grounds that U.S. flange pressure ratings were expressed in pounds per square inch. This is a no-no in international standards since everything has to be metric. H. D. Baumann, then the U.S. delegate to this particular committee had a bright idea and resubmitted the tabulation under a different heading where he replaced the words *pound per square inch* with the word class (i.e., no stated pressures). Thus, a flange rated for 150 psi now was called Class 150. This made the U.S. proposal acceptable, and according to *Business Week*,* saved the U.S. valve industry $3.5 million in retooling costs (in 1971 dollars). Incidentally, the previously accepted dimensions were taken from the German DIN Standard and would have placed the German valve companies at a significant competitive advantage.

Supra National Committees such as the Trilateral Committee, which was chaired for many years by David Rockefeller (of Chase Manhattan Bank), still very much influences the political relationship between the U.S., Europe, Japan and the *Club of Rome*,** which in 1972 decreed that the rate of consumption in the developing countries would lead to disaster and early depletion of raw materials. As a result, we have environmental movements, lead free gasoline, catalytic converters in cars, and a substantial growth in government bureaucracy willfully enlarged to create additional purchasing power to absorb the excess industrial production capacity in the hope of avoiding disruptive business cycles.

What to do about meetings.

There are numerous ways to increase the efficiency of meetings such as by shortening their duration and by running meetings in a more businesslike manner (having a good chairperson). According to Milo C. Frank*, "The difference

---

* *Business Week*, pp. 40, (October 7, 1972)
** *The Economist*, pp. 19 (December 20, 1997)

between a stimulating discussion and a productive meeting is results!"

The best way to run meetings is to have none! The second best way is to have as few as possible. Decisions should be made by the CEO or department heads following input and/or advice from his or her subordinates, but never by a unanimous committee vote. This way he or she can take full credit for a good decision or full blame for a bad one. This is the way it should be.

Why do I discuss meetings at great length? Because in a corporate structure they contribute more than anything else to highly wasteful allocation and use of mostly salaried labor, and to bad business decisions. While decisions derived in committees create consensus (which may be positive), the consensus is derived after considerable time....time that in our ever-faster business cycles becomes a rare commodity. Most Japanese companies were known to run their businesses by the consensus method. No longer. More and more companies can no longer afford this luxury and have discarded this relic from the past. And don't even confuse meetings derived consensus with *teamwork*. While it takes a football *team* to win a game, it is still the individual team member who kicks the field goal!

Here is a tip, when you *must* have a safety or loss prevention committee (because some state governments mandate it),

---

* Frank, Milo C., "How to run a successful meeting in half the time," (New York: Simon & Schuster, 1989).

(a) have as few people as possible participate, and (b) try to have this committee meet only once a year!

As to the number of participants, being a member of a committee is for many people a matter of great prestige, especially when selected from the lower ranks. Therefore, they will do their best to come up with many *solutions* to prove their mettle.

The other problem is meeting sequence. When the committee starts, it is easy to find the obvious shortcomings like, "there is no lighted exit sign over the rear door of warehouse 1," or "the safety guard on the beltsander is broken." However, after the second or third monthly meeting, members are hard pressed to find flaws. Since committees *never* voluntarily disband, and because it looks silly to have minutes of meetings showing no tangible results, problems are invented so solutions can be found! Such as, "let's relocate door No. 2 in Building C so that in case of a fire, we can shorten the escape route." After all, the human mind, and if you have ten members, up to ten human minds, can be very resourceful when it comes to proving its need for existence of this committee.

Now management is between a rock and a hard place. Giving into many superfluous and costly solutions will drain the maintenance staff's labor and will cost a lot of money. To refuse will open up the company to the possibility of a future lawsuit in case, God forbid, some accident happens and the plaintiff's lawyer can prove that management *willfully ignored* most recommendations of the safety committee. You can almost see the angry reaction of any jury to such callous behavior!

The other detriment of ignoring committee recommendations is the adverse results on the morale of the employees.

Therefore, meeting ideally only once a year reduces the number of problems faced by management by a factor of twelve, yet everybody stays happy!

Of course, in the *good old days* before intervention of the all-knowing and all-caring government, you had an inspector from your insurance company come around maybe once a year. He was a trained professional, and he would spot shortcomings, write a report, and management would fix the problem(s) if required. Alas, we don't live in such simple times anymore! We have to do our best to live with the facts of modern life.

Hey, here is a great idea! How about a committee to study and limit the adverse effects of other committees on the fiscal well being of your company?

Chapter 4

THE COMPUTER AND OTHER
FORMS OF MISCOMMUNICATION

The sum of all communication is zero.

The above may sound like a paradox, but it is not. For every message we send out, we expect an answer (at least in theory), bringing the total outstanding messages to zero.

Today, it seems incomprehensible to think World War II was won without a computer, let alone a fax machine or even a simple office copy machine. But it was with an incredible amount of personnel (16.1 million*) and material being moved in two separate parts of the world. The question is, could we duplicate this feat with the vast

---

* Satistical Abstract of the United States, (Washington D.C.: U.S. Dept. of Commerce, 1996).

amount of information technology at our disposal today? The answer is not necessarily an unqualified yes.

Another example is mail delivery. All the automatic sorting equipment and computer systems cannot guarantee same day first class letter delivery say between Boston and New York—a feat that was accomplished with hand sorting and steam locomotives 100 years ago. What we have to realize is that the increase in *information* demands has caused an increase in personnel to handle it, i.e., create and disseminate the information.

E-Mail Mania

In the past, you wrote a letter to Department A, perhaps with a copy to your boss (the number of legible copies a typewriter could handle was definitely limited.) Today, with a click of a button, e-mail allows you to send a letter to the person whom the letter is addressed as well as to a great number of other people simultaneously.

Why do we do it other than because *it is so easy*? First, it shows the world that we are doing our job; secondly, we somehow expect a reply *from other interested parties*, even from as far away as Katmandu! Not receiving e-mail is devastating to the mental well-being of today's managers and is now probably the leading cause of stomach ulcers. The result is a vast proliferation of e-mail messages, which all have to be read because you may be the person to whom it is addressed instead of merely being copied.

Two problems now arise: First, employees spend a great

portion of their supposedly productive hours doing *electronic communication*. Secondly, if people are too busy being productive, as they should be, they ignore e-mail. This is not necessarily good either because there may have been an important and urgent request lurking among the fluff. By in large more and more people write and read e-mail (with gradually increasing grammar and spelling errors if education progresses on its current path). They do this primarily out of fear of appearing computer illiterate or old fashioned. The invariable result is an increase in the total office work hours-translated, more employees.

Under the headlines, "A flood of messages is inundating offices," *The Wall Street Journal** reported on a study sponsored by Pitney Bowes, Inc., which found that e-mail is not replacing other kinds of messages but is *layered over existing methods, increasing the communication load*. They go on to report that some people get more than 150 messages a day! At three minutes each, that adds 7.5 hours to a working day! So where does such a person find time to answer the phone, attend meetings, and lastly, but *most importantly*, do some productive work! What invariably will happen is that such a person will *delegate* some of his or her responsibilities. In plain English, he or she will hire an assistant.

After e-mail started to flourish, companies decided to eliminate secretarial positioners. After all, who needs a secretary if the manager can type his own e-mail. This may be a seemingly justifiable reason for having e-mail with the resultant

---

* *Wall Street Journal*, Tuesday, April 8, 1997, p. B1.

personnel (secretary) savings. However, I suspect otherwise. First of all, only departments or senior management had secretaries and there are, perhaps, 10 e-mail users for each terminated secretarial position. Secondly, if a manager with a $100,000 a year salary types (probably one finger method) his own mail, which may take an average of two hours per day, this will cost his company about $25,000 per year. Compared to the salary of a secretary, this is not much of a savings not counting the more productive work the manager could have been performing during this time.

The greatest accomplishment of Bill Gates and others like him was, in my opinion, to make it fashionable for presidents of large corporations to type their own letters. Just ten years ago they would have thrown you out of their offices if you dared make such a suggestion. Just to show you how ridiculous e-mail-mania has become, one only needs to look around to see that people send e-mail messages to each other even though their offices are within shouting distance!

Phone tag or other office fun

The good old telephone, which served us so well for more than 100 years is getting *modernized*, i.e., adding to the *efficiency* of the office. Ten years ago you could call the sales manager of a vendor company and the company operator would courteously connect you to him. If he were on a trip or in a meeting, you would get to speak to his secretary who would then take a message or would let you know when he would be available. That is no longer true. Now you talk to a computer that asks you to enter the first three letters of a person's name! In most cases, you would not know the sales manager's name (unless you look it up in the Dow Jones® Index). Even if you knew the name, you may be apt to mis-spell it and not get a connection, or the directory list may not be current....after all, under which job description does phone system programmer/manager fall?. Finally, if you are lucky, you may get into his voice mail.

The latter is a fiendish invention by the telephone compa-nies to add untold billions of dollars to their revenues for unneeded and wasteful telephone services.

Voice Mail is nothing but a sexier name for *answering service*. Since the secretary disappeared with the coming of the age of e-mail, there would be nobody to tell you that the person you are seeking to talk to may be on vacation, sick, on a trip, in a meeting, *indisposed*, or fired. What is worse is that peo-ple have gotten so used to having voice mail, they don't even bother to answer the phone when it rings in their office. When they later (if ever) return the call, chances are they only get the voice mail of the first caller, thereby playing a *catch me* game to the huge delight and profit of the telephone companies!

Data explosions

Now onto computers. Computers do a vital task without which we could not support most operations in accounting, engineering, planning, etc. The trouble is computers need software, i.e., a specific set of instructions to perform a given task. Here is where the trouble begins. Software costs make or break an operation. They can perform virtual miracles and create reams of useful data, or they can create chaos requiring endless re-education of workers, constant monitoring and maintenance because of system *crashes*, and, otherwise, can be a bottomless pit in which management spends endless amounts of money to get either different software or hire consultants. A love-hate relationship exists in many companies regarding computer systems. With computer hardware becoming more and more complex, we need System Managers to keep our PC-networks and software running properly, a position that did not exist 15 years ago.

A billion-dollar chip and computer industry exist primarily because they convince us that we always need more memory, or yet, a more powerful computer model. As Marshall McLuhan proclaimed, "The media is the message." The perceived *payback* of capital invested for computers in the eyes of management is to save labor. That is, the expended funds will be recovered in personnel savings. Sadly, this is seldom true.

As pointed out by Stephen Roach*, a Morgan Stanley analyst, there is no evidence that computers actually save labor, taking the economy as a whole! He states that the productivity gains of the information age are just a myth. I can attest to this based on my own, albeit limited, experience. The reason for this seemingly irrational finding is quite simple. In the past, when we compiled statistics or reports by hand using only adding machines, the output was rather

---

* *New Hampshire Sunday News*, Manchester, New Hampshire, August 17, 1997.

limited and the reporting activity was restricted, say, to a monthly P&L statement and a sales statistic, for example. The computer made it easy to add many more reports. System managers, typically beg their *customers* (company department heads) for requests for even more reports to be generated. The reason is simple: having more requests will increase his or her department and stature in the company. I recall one sales manager who requested a monthly sales report on not only what was sold but to whom, including the exact nature of the customer's business, the location, and so on. In small print, this monthly report would be 3 inches thick. The Data Handling Department always placed a new report on the vice president's credenza to be removed next month to make space for the newer report. I never recall seeing him read this report. In any case, it would have taken him several days to do so. He quite simply requested the report because *it could be done*. I am sure he has no idea how much money it cost his company to compile, store, maintain, and process all that data.

Excess investment in automation, of which data systems is part, can lead to a drain in financial resources and efficiencies. If overhead becomes excessive, try to force your competitors to follow your example (and become equally inefficient), otherwise you will find yourself to be no longer competitive and out of business.

A case in point: After supermarkets became the predominant place to do one's shopping, it forced practically all local *mom and pop* grocery stores out of business. That was in the 1960's and 1970's. Since then, supermarkets have invested heavily in automating their inventory control and checkout systems (most notably barcode reading equipment). The result was a steady escalation of grocery prices to pay for the required extra capital. The unforeseen and surprising results is that local convenience stores are back in business and are thriving!

In his book, *The Great Boom Ahead**, Harry Dent states: "We have put computers to work to make our huge bureaucratic staffs a little more efficient-word processing, accounting, financial spreadsheets, and so on! The least investment has gone into our sales and customer service personnel, the very people who affect our customers the most. This is why our investments in computerization in the 70's and 80's produced such minor productivity gains." Well said, and may I add, "—and in the 90's too!"

---

* Dent, Harry, *The Great Boom Ahead*, (New York: Hyperion, 1993).

Chapter 5

COMPUTER SOFTWARE

Advances in computer programming barely keep up
with the increase in illiteracy of the general population.

Software is to computers what gasoline is to automobiles—
without it, nothing runs. Aside from general software programs that allow you to type a letter or set up a simple balance sheet, managers of companies need very sophisticated
programs that can run an entire company operation including sales, order entry, manufacturing, engineering, purchasing, and accounting just to name a few basic departments.

The function of each of these departments, or functional
blocks within a company organization, evolved usually
over many years of growth and continual adjustments to,
hopefully, make it more efficient and productive. This all
added some complexity to the organization. The result is
that very few people, if any, can tell you the exact workflow,
the reasons for doing certain things, and explain the overall

34

departmental system. If things get that complicated on the department level, what do you think happens on the over-all company level with perhaps 12 to 15 departments? There is probably no CEO alive who can explain the exact route a customer order takes from the incoming fax or call to the invoice being mailed to the customer.

You now expect an outside software company to duplicate this system, which exists only in the heads of perhaps 100 different people, and to put it into programming language for a company-wide computer system. This is practically an impossible task and exactly the crux of the problem encoun-tered by many CEOs. Problems that brought many compa-nies to the brink of bankruptcy.

There are only two ways of *automating* company wide sys-tems. The first, and preferred way, is to purchase good commercially available software. One that is able to com-bine word processing and data-handling capabilities. You then use a bright software engineer, preferably from your own company (so he is familiar with your work) and have him modify or adapt this *canned* software to duplicate as much as possible the exact way your individual depart-ments currently operate. It is absolutely essential to estab-lish exactly what the software should do *before* any soft-ware coding begins. This should be done in writing with everybody concerned *signing off* on it. Resist all tempta-tions to *load-up* the software with unnecessary reports and functions! Unfortunately, doing only this much is already quite complex and you may only be able to do it by indi-vidual departments. Nevertheless, try to set the software up so it can accept data input from one department to the next (saving redundancy thereby cutting costs and errors). If everything goes well, you eventually have a company-wide data processing system that runs smoothly and requires hardly any training of the people involved. After all, they are doing the same work as before except now they are working on a PC or workstation instead of doing it by, say, a typewriter. Nevertheless, even this takes lots of time and training.

One thing that is absolutely essential—don't switch over from a manual to a computer system immediately. Work both systems in parallel for at least six months. Make sure the program is thoroughly debugged. Even if things run smoothly, don't discard the old manual forms or typewriters quite yet. They may come in handy when the system *crashes*.

The above, in my opinion, is the only way to *computerize* a company system; however, there is another way. This typically is an evolved *enterprise* system which not only requires elaborate hardware but which requires very expensive software. The six or seven digit software cost is only the tip of the iceberg. According to an article in the *Wall Street Journal** describing a popular German R/3® software program: "Companies must play host to armies of consultants who sometimes charge as much as five times what the software itself cost and can stay on the job for years." They cite Owens-Corning Fiberglass Corp. for

---

* *Wall Street Journal*, March 14, 1997, p. B1.

paying between $15 to $20 million for their R/3 project.

The above mentioned consultants are needed for explaining to and training your employees on how the *new* system works. You have to understand that in order to use such software, you have to adapt the way you used to do business to the new way dictated by the *outside* system. This is tantamount to redesigning your company from the ground up....everything runs differently. It involves months of organizational upheaval, shuffling of personnel, untold near or actual nervous breakdowns, vast amounts of costly man hours due to retraining, and so on. This also does not include the lost orders, reduced company image, upset customers, etc.

Municipal governments are even bigger victims of what sometimes amounts to software fraud. As a headline in the March 21, 1997 issue of the *Palm Beach Post* reported: "Unneeded software cost the county $2.8 million including $1.04 million on maintenance."

Alas, if everything is done right and after spending untold millions of dollars, at the touch of a button the CEO will know *in real time* the up to the second amounts of orders in house. Wow!

One thing you have to realize is the sophisticated software programs discussed above tend to revolve around the Accounting Department and its requirements (see Fig. 1). No wonder, because some of the software programs were created by accounting firms such as Price-Waterhouse. To me, this is a perversion of the order of importance. By far the most important portion of any manufacturing organization is order fulfillment, or the manufacturing system (see Fig. 2). If this system works well, your customers are happy and you make a profit. To balance the books is of secondary importance. If everything else fails, you can always call your banker and see if the cash in your bank account is growing—a sure sign that you are making money. If not, then you are in trouble....with or without fancy software.

There is the tempting logic to center software around the accounting requirements. After all, nearly everything can be

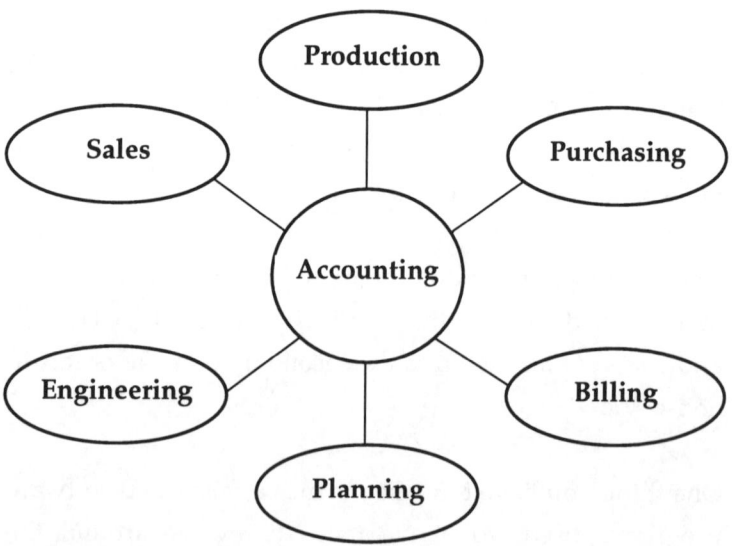

Figure 6-1: Example of Accounting-centered enterprise software.

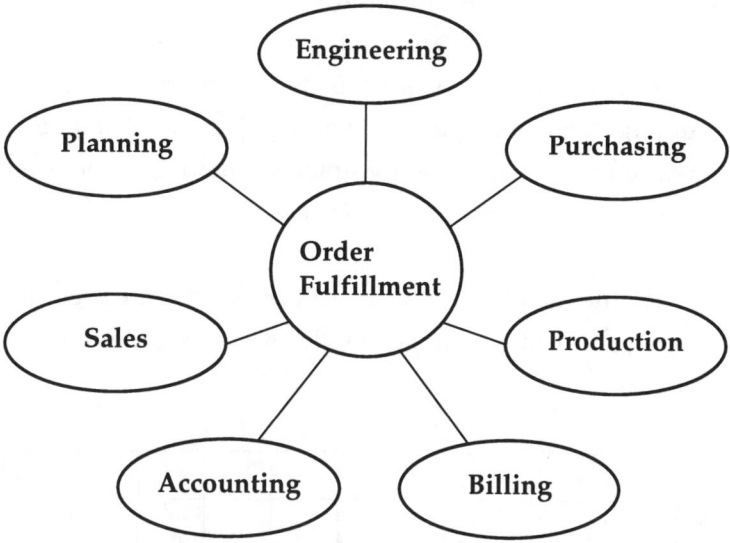

Figure 6-2: A more rational manufacturing system-centered enterprise software.

expressed in terms of money (cost, inventory, sales, etc.). However, such a system will certainly force you to redesign all of your company's vital operations in order to comply with the demands of such software.

I know of a pump company who used a standard cost system in the past that consisted of groups of product lines and sizes with some adjustments for variations thrown in. This cost accounting system was so effective, that the difference between the book value of the inventory to the value of the physical count was always less than 1%!

The new software program required that a different Bill of

Material* be generated for each, separate pump (even if it differed from a "standard" pump by only a primer coat). The result was an excess of 10,000 Bills of Materials and still counting. The only persons not complaining about this waste of money are the new employees hired to generate all these new documents.

On the other hand, a production-centered software program allows you to adapt and keep your present system more or less intact.

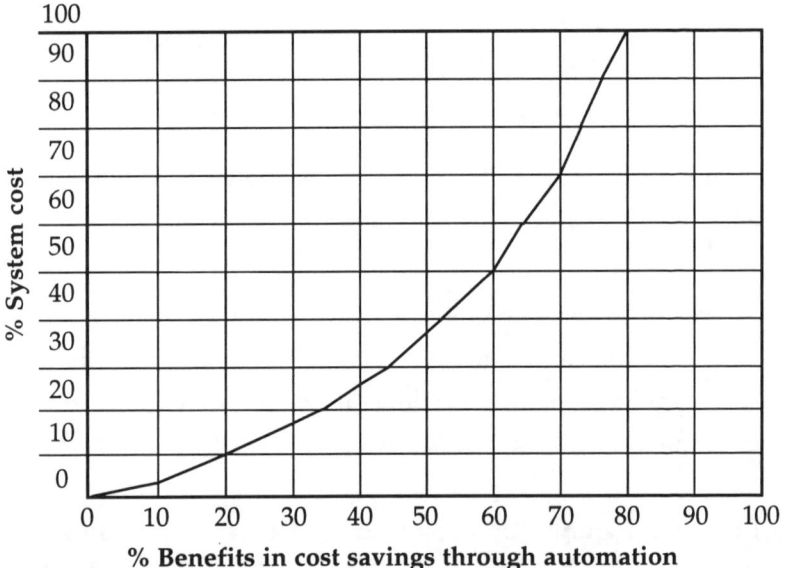

FIGURE 5,3
Typical Cost Benefit Relationship between computer plus software cost and percentage of perceived benefits through system automation. Note: at 80% benefits cost already exceeds 100%! Optimal benefits lie around 60%. Don't ever try to reach 100% automation.

---

* A listing of all separate parts required to build a complete assembly, in this case, a pump.

Chapter 6

Running an Enterprise Government Style

Taxes expand to cover Government's Losses.

We may belittle inefficient government agencies or enterprises when they are run so badly because it has been reported so often that we are numb to it. It is true that any inefficiency will always be covered up by tax money, contrary to private enterprise where bankruptcy is the inevitable end of such folly (except if a business has a monopoly in a given service or product). In the latter case, a price increase will cover up bad management. It is our fault as citizens to let inefficient government happen. The cover-up starts with the local Chamber of Commerce trying not to *rock the boat* knowing quite well that the closure of a facility will be bad for local businesses. It extends to unions afraid to lose members and, therefore, income. The next groups of people to keep this under the table are the congressmen, senators, and governors who are all afraid to lose votes if workers are laid off or the local economy is going to be hurt.

Inefficient government businesses are kept running sometimes without any real purpose (the same can be said of some departments of larger private companies). A case in point: My factory was located not too far from a Navy shipyard which overhauls (repairs) one, or sometimes, two, nuclear submarines. This Yard used to employ 8,200 full-time plus 800 *part-time* workers. The last element was a ploy by the Yard's management to pull the wool over Congress's eyes. These 800 employees would be hired two months before the budget review process. Then four months later, these employees would be laid off as a sign of *good will* towards Congress (See how efficient we are? We promise to do the same job by saving 10% of the workforce—"applause"). The local papers even advertised in their help wanted ads that these part time jobs were only to last six months. This ploy worked for many years!

When guests would visit the company, sometimes I would take them out of town to a restaurant within view of the Navy Yard. Pointing out the facilities and explaining their functions, I gave my guests a test of sorts. I asked them to guess how many workers they thought it would take to repair two nuclear submarines taking into consideration that hardly more than 50 persons could *work* in such tight surroundings without bumping into each other. I also cautioned them to consider that the yard is not a moneymaking enterprise, but a Government-run facility. The answers from the mostly very experienced people (some company presidents themselves) ranged in numbers from 300 to a maximum of 1,200 employees. They were stunned when I told them the true number was 8,200!

With the end of the cold war and the decommissioning of many submarines, the Yard finally has had to make some cutbacks, and the current employment stands around 3,800 (there was not a single submarine in the Yard the previous year). So aside from paying all these people for political or social reasons, what do all of these people do? The answer may surprise you. They are all very busy!

Here is a breakdown of the various major departments and the labor as of 1996:

Department	Number of Employees
Engineers (quality and process)	296
Administration & Accounting	605
Electronic Data System	358
Training and Education	225
Public Relations	53
Machine Shop	278
Power Plants	136
Yard facilities	120
Maintenance	178
Human Resources	203
Security (other than U.S. Marine guard)	58
Navy Liaison	125
Congressional Liaison	37
Procurement	413

Department	Number of Employees
Communication	62
Print Shop	112
Warehousing/Storage	155
Yard workforce (people who actually perform work inside a submarine)	395
TOTAL	**3,809**

As you can see, everybody is not only gainfully employed but also very busy with some overtime thrown in to make up for time lost due to vacation and illnesses. This, of course, does not take into account the occasional goof-off who hides in the supply room to read *Playboy®Magazine.*

Now, I hasten to say that the above organizational chart is entirely the product of my imagination knowing quite well that this type of data is highly classified. The last thing I need is the F.B.I. knocking on my door.

The work you and I may consider non-productive is of very high value to the affected employees. Consider, for example, the three-year study of the Engineering Department on how to increase efficiency at the Yard. The outcome of these many thousands of man hours was a new procedure whereby a yard worker would look up the drawing for a given piece of equipment and *then* go inside the submarine to take the part out. In the old system, they would go inside the submarine, look at the part, and then go and get the drawing. I kid you not!

Consider the machinist I once hired from the Navy Yard. He

was assigned to a gear hobbing machine*. Like his counter-part during the day shift, he actually does not perform any work other than stand by *in case* somewhere in the world a propulsion gear breaks. A *code red* would be related to the Yard by radio, which would then cause the worker to push the *start* button on his machine. Placing a spare gear in the warehouse would do no good. Since gears break very infre-quently, chances are that this spare gear would lay on the shelf for more than one year, and under Navy regulations, equipment that is not used within a year is to be discarded. So you see, it makes perfectly good sense to pay people to do nothing!

It has not always been this way. During World War II, the Yard was one of the most efficient production facilities for diesel powered submarines. If we go back farther, we find a very dramatic increase in the ratio between effective and administrative personnel. For example, according to a report in the *Army and Navy Chronicle*,** dated 8/20/1840, the bud-get of the French Navy was listed as: 7,539,700 Francs for officers; 19,066,000 Francs for enlisted men, and only 666,500 Francs for administrative personnel, or only 2.4% of the total are administrative personnel expenses!

In his famous book, *Parkinson's Law*,*** C.N. Parkinson related that in the British Navy dockyards the number of

---

* A machine to cut teeth into a gear used in this case to drive the propeller.

** *Army and Navy Chronicle*, (Washington, D.C, 1840)

*** Parkinson, C.N., *Parkinson's Law*, (Boston: Houghton Mifflin Co., 1975) administrative personnel grew from 5.7% of the total in 1914 to 7.3% in 1928—an increase of 28% in 14 years. The trend to increase the administrative number of employees seems to have accelerated in more recent times, perhaps due to the demands of increasing communications (after all, in 1914, there was only Morse code, now we have e-mail). Anyhow, Parkinson found that the British staff of the colonial office, for example, increased by an average of 5.89% per year between 1935 and 1954. This, despite the fact that most of the colonies gained independence during this period.

What does this all mean to us as businesspersons? Well, if thousands of people can exist in Government toiling to communicate, teach, support, and otherwise keep each other occupied, then the same can happen, perhaps on a smaller scale, within certain departments of private companies.

Isn't it remarkable that following massive lay-offs in the U.S. industry during and after the last recession (1992), the profit of most of those companies exploded, which in turn led to one of the biggest bull markets the United States has ever had. Internal vigilance by management and tight control of the budget are needed to avoid such uncontrolled growth in bureaucracy that, like a cancer, can destroy a healthy organization from within.

Don't be fooled by the fact that all employees in a given department are working hard. The only question is: Does their work produce profit? As you can see from the above example of the Navy Yard, the only *effective* employees are those 395 people actually doing the repair work (10.4% of the total). Yet, the Yard would still exist and everybody would still be working eight hours a day if those 395 effective employees were to be laid off! This is the lesson we can draw from such an organization: The size of an organization or department has nothing to do with the stated purpose, or as C.N. Parkinson so eloquently stated: "Work expands to fill the time available."

Chapter 7

Small is Beautiful,
or the Law of the Sphere

*Increases in manufacturing efficiency barely keep up with
the increase in administrative expenses.*

To paraphrase the old saying: "If you are not a liberal under
30, you have no heart; if you are not a conservative over 40,
you have no brain." I propose: "If you don't believe in a centralized corporate structure under 30, you flunked your
MBA exams; if you don't believe in a decentralized organization by the time you are 40, then don't start a business!"

While never having attended a business school, I nevertheless was enthralled by the seemingly obvious economics of large combined corporate structures when I was a
young man. After all, a large corporation has more corporate resources and a well-staffed R&D Department than a
small company, not to mention the big clout of its corporate

marketing and sales staff. In addition, you have the centralized purchasing power to put all kinds of cost cutting pressure on your vendors.

When I got older and had practical exposure to the ways smaller and larger companies worked, I found that similar to large central governments, any technical efficiencies achieved by greater size were eaten away by the *human factor*. By *human factor* I mean the resultant impersonalization of the individual employee, the stifling inefficiencies of multi-layered management, and worst of all, by the constant attempts by middle management to accumulate staff and to build empires.

When debating the issue of small vs. large companies, one must distinguish between two categories of employees.

1. *The effective* employee
2. The *supportive* employee

Note that I use the term *effective* instead of *efficient*. To make my point, a manager working in the Environmental Service Department of a large corporation might be very efficient in writing letters to the Federal Government outlining plans to avoid spills, but this effort is not effective in increasing sales and, therefore, profit (this does not imply the job is not necessary, after all, a fine by the government can be costly and bad public relations!).

For the purpose of this study, I will categorize those employees whose work is not directly related to sales and production as *supportive*. This category would include employees in departments such as Research and Development, Marketing, Public Relations, Human Resources, Stockholder Relations, and others of this sort.

In his book, *The Dilbert Principle,** Scott Adams defines *non-fundamental work* (done by supportive staff) as:

Quality fair	Employee satisfaction survey
Process improvement team	Suggestion system
Recognition committee	ISO 9000
Standards	Reorganization
Policy improvement	Budget process
Writing vision statements	Writing an *approved*
Writing mission statements	*equipment list*

He further defined *non-fundamental work* as: "any activity that is one level removed from your people or your product."

In looking at the above table, most sensible people would readily agree that the majority of the stated activities are not necessary and usually the result of popular fads. However, the larger the company, the more unnecessary activities are tolerated.

It is difficult to measure the output of employees who work in supportive departments, which is usually related to the effectiveness of their supervisor. Such effectiveness is impaired if (1) there is not enough backup work (not

---

* Scott Adams, "The Dilbert Principle," (Harper Collins), 1996.

knowing what to do when my current work assignment is completed will produce *rubber work*, or, again, in the words of C.N. Parkinson*: "Work expands to fill the time available," and (2) if the supervisor does not have the technical background to understand the work he assigns (he is at the mercy of his staff and has to believe in all real or imaginary problems that a given project encounters).

Strictly considering the direct impact on the business performance of a company, effective employees are personnel involved in direct sales support, production, including direct production supervision, planning and purchasing (strictly related to business inventories), and engineering personnel involved in order related efforts. In other words, an effective employee is any person whose effort leads directly to obtaining and executing a customer order and whose effort, therefore, has a direct impact on the profitability of the enterprise.

As you can see, my examples are related to manufacturing companies where the distinction can most readily be made. (However, a similar analysis should apply to other businesses as well.)

A good manager is interested in having a high ratio of *effective* to *supportive* employees in his company, or a high E/S ratio. Achieving this is your ticket to profitability. I strongly believe that control of the E/S ratio is the most important

---

* C. Northote Parkinson, "Parkinson's Law," (Boston: Houghton Mifflin Co.), 1975.

task of any chief executive officer. Growth in the *effective* category is usually business related. If order volume increases, you first work overtime and later hire more personnel. This is a relatively easy task and the whole process is nearly transparent. On the other hand, when orders decrease, such as in a recession, you reverse the process. First, you reduce working hours, and then you terminate positions. Unfortunately, the latter typically does not happen in the *supportive* category. Terminating supportive positions usually is an act of desperation, i.e., when times are tough and the balance sheet is awash in red ink. Why is this true? Well one of the reasons is that staff positions tend to become *invisible* compared to hourly wages and widgets produced per hour. There are endless business studies on how to improve efficiencies in production, but hardly any on how to improve *efficiencies* of staff people. How does one measure the efficiency of a marketing person? If it took ten people to come up with a brand name for a *new and improved* detergent, could five persons do just as well? Probably.

In my past association with medium-sized manufacturing companies, I was absolutely astonished to see management hire consultants to time study the performance of the machine shop to determine the machining time of individual parts expressed in minutes to the fourth decimal place! This was done even though the union workers made a point of slowing down the normal machine tool speed upon spotting such a time keeper.

We have this tremendous fascination to reduce direct labor (typically 18% of the selling price) by 5% or 10%, but we think nothing of increasing General and Administrative (G&A) expenses by 5% (hiring time keepers, increase planning staff., etc.) in order to do this. Incidentally, a 10% *decrease* in direct labor increases profit by about 1.8% while a 5% increase in G&A decreases profit by 2.%—a net loss of 0.2%!

The latest trend in *reducing cost* is to relocate machining facilities from the United States to other countries such as Mexico, Eastern Europe, and Asia. The reason is most managers are fascinated by the direct wage differential, i.e., $15 per hour in Nebraska versus $3.00 per hour in Mexico. This is a very superficial comparison. Since practically all modern tool machines are numerically controlled, their cost is rather high (several hundred thousand dollars each); therefore, the cost of the machine alone is typically $40.00 per hour due to depreciation of the purchase price alone. The real comparison between Mexico and the U.S. is, therefore, $40 + $3 versus $40 + $15, or a 22% cost saving instead of 80%...still not too bad. However, to that you have to add the cost of building a new plant, training your employees (a typically high turnover in Mexico), relocating U.S. supervisors (at higher salaries), increased transportation costs, and such mundane items such as finding trained mechanics to service the electronics. Relocating assembly operations, requiring essentially low cost manual labor with fewer expensive machine tools, makes much more sense. Nevertheless, all these relocation studies consume an awful lot of staff work and travel expenses. *Supportive* cost that is typically not accounted for in the *cost cutting* planning stage!

Returning to the problem of maintaining a decent ratio of *effective* to *supportive* personnel. One of the biggest problems a CEO faces is determining the optimum, or better yet, the *absolute minimum* number of staff or supportive personnel needed in the organization. This is a daunting task and gets more difficult the larger a company is, i.e., the organizational structure becomes less and less *transparent* with an increase in size. Relying on your department heads in this matter is usually futile. Typical statements will be, "We are already cut to the bone." "We even had more employees during the '82 depression," or "Our Marketing Department is smaller than competitor X. If we reduce our staff further, we will not be able to introduce new products," etc.

The trend in electronic communications will also tend to increase staff requirements. After all, somebody has to read all the extra reports that computers generate. All this is a clear argument for decentralization and smaller-sized companies. Remind yourself that small is beautiful and small is profitable. If nothing else, it restores the transparency of a company's organizational structure to the eyes of the CEO.

Consider the chart in Figure 8-1. It contains plotted performance data for metal fabricating and machining industries taken from *Value Line*®* for the year 1994. I excluded companies with sales over $1 billion since those companies are typically conglomerates of many smaller, quasi-independent companies and, therefore, would not be representative for this study. On the other hand, companies

---

* *Value Line*®, Value Line Publishing Inc., 1994.

below $100 million were not listed and, therefore, are not included.

The graph demonstrates two things: First, it is amazing how many companies are satisfied with a profit B.I.T. of only 5% to 10%. Apparently their measure of success is to be comparable to their competitors. Second, this chart shows a definite trend towards higher profit with decreasing sales, i.e., smaller company size. For example, the average profit for companies with between $500 million and $1,000 million in sales is 6.17%, for those between $250 and $500 million it's 8.4%, and between $100 to $250 million it's 11.6%!

One of the problems encountered with larger sized companies is the number of layers of management. In his excellent book, *Thriving in Chaos**, Tom Peters suggests limiting the number of management layers to no more than five, with between 25 to 75 people reporting to a manager. Except for manufacturing or purely clerical jobs, (such as data entry in an insurance company), I personally consider more than 25 persons to be non-manageable for one manager.

Let's consider an industrial company and forget the Manufacturing Department, which is usually not the problem in any organization. There are typically ten departments such as Sales, Marketing, Order Entry, Engineering, Research and Development, Human Resources, Purchasing, Planning, Accounting, and Customer Service as a minimum. Assuming each is staffed with 25 people, there would be 250

---

* Thomas Peters, "Thriving in Chaos," (New York: A. Knopf), 1987

plus 10 managers equaling 260 employees, not including the CEO. This would be a three-layer company. If the company is larger, we find 25 sub-sections in each of the ten major departments of 25 people each. This would bring the company up to four management layers and the head count (not adding the manufacturing labor) to $\{[(25 + 1) \times 25] + 25\} \times 10 + 10$ department heads and 1 CEO = 6,761 employees. After adding the CEO, this would be the absolute largest company with a five-layer structure.

However, the reality is that there are typically only four to twelve persons reporting to one supervisor or manager. Using an average size of eight per department and with a maximum layer of five management levels, we have to limit the size of the non-manufacturing portion of any company to only $\{[(8 + 1) \times 8] + 8\} \times 8 + 8$ and 1 CEO = 649 employees! There are then only two ways to increase the company's size: (1) Increase the number of layers of management, or (2) split the company into several smaller, *autonomous*, divisions, i.e., the division should operate all but in name as a completely separate company unfettered by the corporate staff!

Emerson Electric Corporation is one of those companies that has successfully kept their divisions independent. The financial results reflect the success of this effort. As their 1996 earning statement proves, with $11,150 million in sales, they achieved a respectable 14.4% profit before taxes, which referring to Figure 8-1, would place them somewhere in the earning range of a single company with about $150 million sales volume.

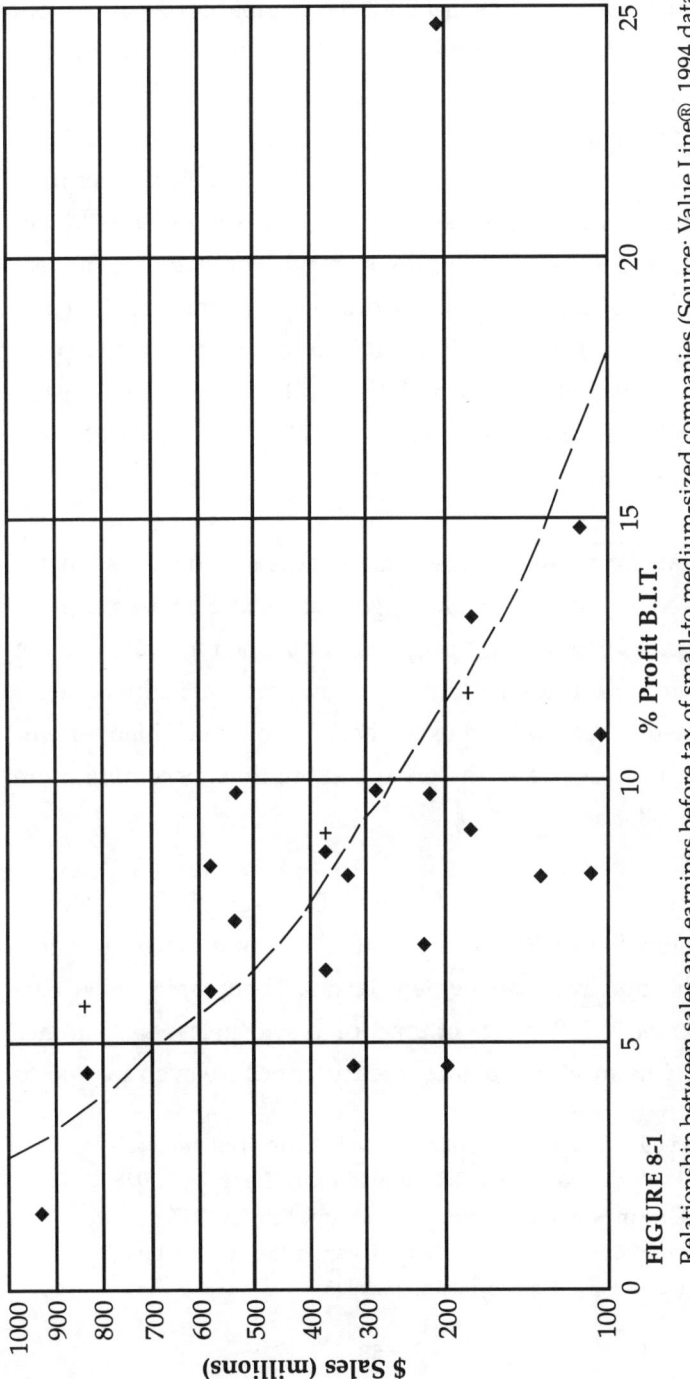

FIGURE 8-1

Relationship between sales and earnings before tax of small-to medium-sized companies (Source: Value Line®, 1994 data)

+ = Average values — = Calculated averages — where % profit = $4(1000/Sales)^{2/3}$

The implied relationship between company size and profit extends also to separate divisions or different manufacturing facilities of larger enterprises. For example, from unpublished financial data of two similar companies in essentially the same business, I found that in company *A*, a larger division with 730 employees had a profit margin (before tax) of 2.7% while their smaller division with only 200 employees had a profit margin of 9.5% during the same year. In company *B*, the large division had 2,300 employees with a profit margin (before tax) of 8.3%, while the smaller division with 1,300 employees achieved 19%, again in the same business year.

To call for smaller, leaner organizations is, of course, nothing new. In his book, *Organization and Management in Industry and Business*,* originally published in 1928, William B. Cornell (incidentally, a fellow mechanical engineer) argued for centralized executive control which inadvertently limits the size of the organization; thus, becoming more controllable.

There are exceptions, of course. For example, the Catholic Church hierarchy manages 407, 750 priests worldwide** with only five management layers. Then again, they have had nearly 2000 years of practice. Nevertheless, as Hammer and Champy*** explain, when you need eleven people to

---

* Cornell, William B., *Organization and Management in Industry and Business*, (New York: The Ronald Press Company), 1928.
** Welt Am Sonntag, Hamburg, Germany, Feb. 23 1997.
*** Hammer and Champy, "Reengineering the Corporation," (New York: Harper Business), 1996.

produce 100 widgets a day, you need 193 people in order to produce 1,000 widgets due to the added support staff (instead of 110). Consider the United States Navy. A typical aircraft carrier needs 5,000 personnel to bring 80 aircraft into action, in other words, it needs more than 60 support people per plane.

An example of how a reduction in layers of management will increase efficiency is given by Tichy and Sherman* who reported that General Electric's Lighting Division reduced its layers of management from seven to four with a resultant increase of sales per salaried employee of 35%!

Considering all that, wouldn't it be nice to have a mathematical tool to predict the relationship between size and profitability? A method that would predict the decrease in profit level when increasing the size of an organization?

Microorganisms found out that smaller is better. Cells, like bacteria, are incredibly small creatures. Evolution, despite all the other changes that have taken place over the millennia, has kept them that small. The reason is that they basically constitute a sphere. The core of the sphere contains just the basic elements for survival and procreation. No extra frills, yet they need a large surface area to interact with other cells or substances. A small diameter gives you that advantage. You lose this advantage the larger the sphere gets.

---

* Tichy and Sherman, "Control Your Destiny or Someone Else Will," (Harper Collins), 1995.

Consider if you will the two spheres in Figures 8-2. The smaller one has a radius of 1-inch while the larger sphere has a radius of 2 inches. The equations governing the surface area of a sphere, A, and the volumes of a sphere, V, are given as follows:

$$A = 4 \times \pi \times R^2 \text{ , or } A = 12.56 \, R^2$$
$$V = 4/3 \times \pi \times R^3 \text{ , or } V = 4.19 \, R^3$$

These equations show that the volume, or the contents of the interior of the sphere, increases to the third power of the radius R. A much faster rate than the increase in the surface area A of a sphere, which only increases to the square of the radius R. Then the volume of the sphere with a 2" radius is eight times larger than that of the 1" radius sphere. Yet the area increased only four times going from a 1" to a 2" radius.

Another example is shown in Figure 8-3. At a radius of 1/2 inch (diameter of 1 inch), for example, the volume happens to be about 0.52 cubic inches and the surface area is 3.14 square inches (a ratio of about 6:1). At 5-inch radius (10-inch diameter), the volume increased to 524 cubic inches while the surface area only increased to 314in^2 (now the ratio is only 0.6:1). This proves that the volume (after increasing the radius ten times) increased 1,000 times while the surface area only increased 100 times! No wonder bacteria want to stay small! They need a relatively large surface area to interact with adjacent cells still utilizing a minimum core (support structure). The natural limit in the size of a bacterium is governed by the ability of the surface area to feed the core substance (the volume).

The above examples show that the relationship between area

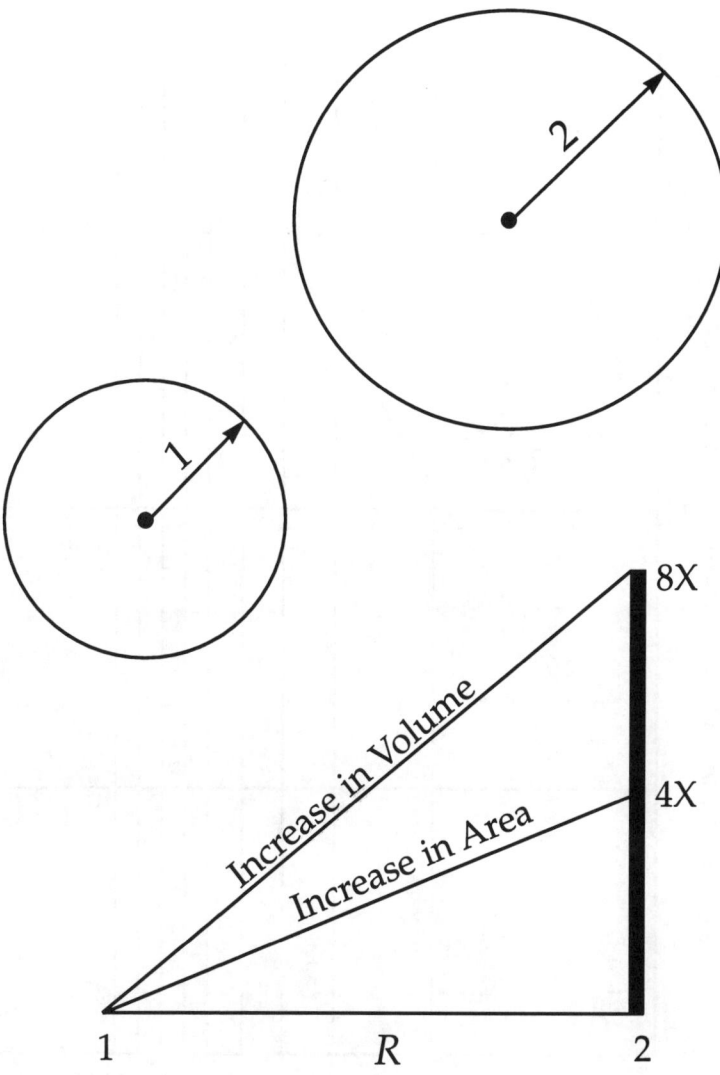

FIGURE 8-2
Relationship between size, volume, and surface area of differently sized spheres.

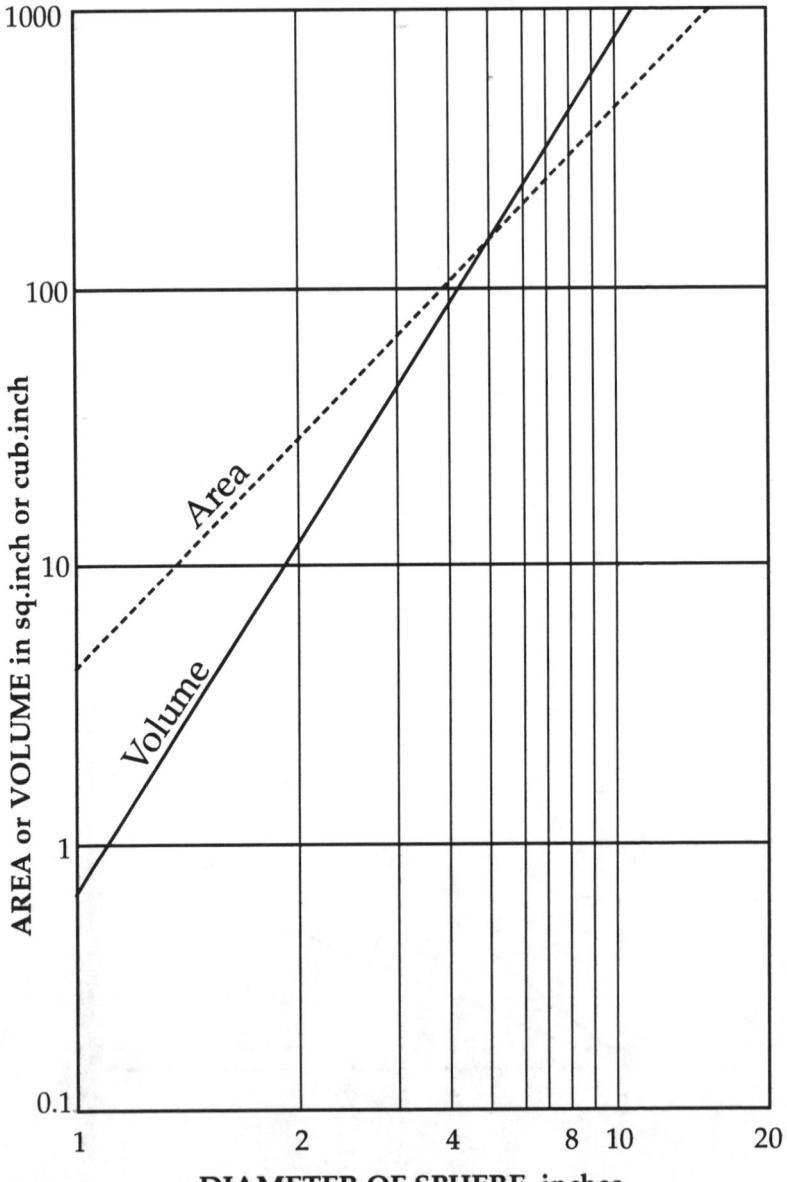

FIGURE 8-3

Example of how the rate of change between the volume and surface diverges.

increase and volume increase is given by $R^{2/3}$, or what I call "the Law of the Sphere."

What I suspect is that human organizations are also subject to this Law of the Sphere. We may compare the surface area of a sphere to that part of an organization that is actively involved in creating profit such as the external sales force engaging the customer if you are a sales organization, or if the organization is an army, engaging the enemy. In manufacturing, the surface area would include: order fulfillment, direct production labor, and so on. In other words, what I previously defined as an effective labor force.

The volume of the sphere, on the other hand, would comprise the total number of employees, including the previously identified *supportive* personnel. In private industry, this would be Corporate Headquarters, Marketing, R&D, stockholder relations, etc., in addition to Manufacturing and Sales. In the army, this would include staff and logistics, for example. Same as bacteria, a good CEO wants a surface area as large as possible compared to the unavoidable volume. This, of course, predicates a small sphere (small organization).

Does such a *Law of the Sphere*, which tells us that the surface area only increases to the two-thirds power of the volume increase, really apply to human organizations? If so, then it would follow that the effective number of employees E_1 out of a given number of total employees T_1 would increase to E_2 by the two-thirds power of the ratio between the total new number of employees T_2 to the old number T_1, or $E_2 = E_1(T_2 /T_1)^{2/3}$. In analyzing data accumulated from private sources and from business publications, I found that such a relationship exists, which while not as mathematically perfect as spheres, may be used to shed light on why organizations seem to lose their efficiency as they get larger.

For example, if the company had a total employment T_1 of 100 people, out of which 60 people E_1 would be in the *effective* category, and you wanted to double the size of the company to 200 people T_2. The new number of *effective* personnel would only increase to: $E_2 = 60 \times (200/100)^{2/3} = 95$ people instead of $2 \times 60 = 120$ people, as you might have guessed. As a matter of fact, in order to double the production, i.e., have 120 effective personnel, you have to increase the size of the firm to 285 people!

Let's get more specific and define the *The Law of the Sphere*: From the previous area to volume relationship, $A_2/A_1 = (V_2/V_1)^{2/3}$, where the area of a second sphere is proportional to the area of a first sphere as given by the two-thirds power of the ratio between the volumes of the second to that of the first sphere. This can now be generalized as:

THE LAW OF THE SPHERE

The ratio between a number depending on a second variable to a number depending on a first variable is given by the two-thirds power of the ratio between the second and the first variable, or somewhat simplified: The ratio of one set of numbers is equal to the two-third's power or the ratio of a second set of numbers:

$$A_2/A_1 = (V_2/V_1)^{2/3}$$

Now if we want to know what A_2 is, we rearrange the equation as follows:

$$A_2 = A_1 (V_2/V_1)^{2/3}$$

Now let's apply this law to human organizations by substituting, for example, the number of total workers for volume and the number of effective workers for area. We now can determine the ratio between the two if a company grows, i.e., the total number of workers increases from size (1) to size (2). So we may state:

$$\frac{\text{No. of effective workers (2)}}{\text{No. of effective workers (1)}} = \frac{[\text{No. of total workers (2)}]^{2/3}}{[\text{No. of total workers (1)}]}$$

Instead of dealing with individual persons, we may substitute a group of workers, such as a department. We, thus, could say there are 12 total departments including 7 effective departments in Plant 1 and 20 total departments in Plant 2. What would be the number of effective departments in Plant 2? The solution is:

$$7(20 / 12)^{2/3} = 9.84 \text{ or rounded to 10 effective departments.}$$

If we want to apply this law to the military (and we may as well), it is easy to substitute the number of effective units, such as companies or divisions for plant departments.

At present there are approximately 495,000* men and

---

* *The New York Times*, April 29, 1997.

women who serve in the U.S. Army. Let's assume the largest, *effective* fighting organization is a Division (about 14,000 soldiers). At first, we would think that the total Division number is 495,000 soldiers divided by 14,000, which equals about 35. However, this is not true, as we shall see later; therefore, let's consult the *Law of the Sphere*.

The total number of Divisions, "X" that can be fielded according to this Law are: $X = 1 \times (495{,}000/14{,}000)^{2/3} = 10.8$ Divisions. This compares well with recent press reports that the U.S., at present, has 10 combat-ready divisions. The above relationship sadly indicates that simply doubling the size of the Army would not double the number of combat-ready divisions. It would only increase it to: $X = 1 \times (990{,}000/14{,}000)^{2/3} = 17.1$ or 17 divisions (rounded off) instead of $2 \times 10.8 =$ about 22! If we multiply the 10.8 Divisions by 14,000 personnel each, we get 151,200 fighting personnel out of a total of 495,000, or one out of 3.3. Contrast this to the ancient Chinese army*, which in about 400 B.C. had three fighting men out of every four.

You may think, well, this is the government—-private industry is much more efficient. Perhaps not always. Consider, for example, the German Volkswagen Company. Ferdinand Porsche designed the original *Beetle* Volkswagen between 1934 and 1936, had the first prototype on the road in 1936, and the first production run of 30 cars assembled by April 1937. This, with about 50 techni-

---

* Sun Tzu, *The Art of War*, (Oxford University Press, 1963) p 72.

cians and engineers and at a cost (at today's dollars) of about $23 million.*

In the 1970s, the Volkswagen Company employed about 50,000 engineers and technicians. Despite this, the company was unable to design a suitable replacement for the then obsolete *Beetle*. In desperation, VW then purchased a German competitor, Auto Union and utilizing the "NSU" Construction, sold it under the name of Rabbit. It was curious, but you could still see the Auto Union's *Olympic Rings* trademark on the car engines produced by VW during the first two years. Why should this be? Consider the law of the sphere. By increasing the engineering staff from 50 to 50,000, Volkswagen Company only increased the number of *effective* engineers by $(50,000/50)^{2/3}= 100$ times-apparently this was not enough. Besides the resultant inefficiency of large numbers of personnel, there is the added handicap of trying to design a car by committees.

Obviously, some companies might be more efficient than others and may be able to maintain a higher ratio of effective to supportive labor than indicated by the mathematical relationship of a pure sphere. However, I maintain that it will be impossible for even the best manager to maintain a *constant* E/S ratio when his company grows. What he may be able to do is maintain a larger exponential growth factor. Table 8-1 shows the mathematical relationship assuming the worst or basic exponent factor of 2/3 dictated by the *Law of the Sphere*

---

* Mommsen, Hans, "Das Volkswagenwerk und Seine Arbeiter im dritten Reich," *Econ Verlag*, 1966.

TABLE 8-1

Relationship between increases in effective labor to overall employment

A) Standard efficiency organization, n=2/3 per the *Law of the Sphere*

Relationship between increases in effective labor to overall employment

If total employment is increased by a factor of:	2	5	10	20	50	100
Then effective labor increases by a factor of:	1.6	2.9	4.6	7.4	13.6	21.5

B) Better efficiency organization, n = 3/4

If total employment is increased by a factor of:	2	5	10	20	50	100
Then effective labor increases by a factor of:	1.7	3.3	5.6	9.5	18.8	31.6

C) Optimum efficiency organization, n = 7/8

If total employment is increased by a factor of:	2	5	10	20	50	100
Then effective labor increases by a factor of:	1.8	4.1	7.5	13.8	30.7	56.2

as previously discussed (A) or a factor of $3/4$ (B), *better*, or if you are really *tops*, then you may manage a $7/8$ factor (C).

As you can see, there has to be a dramatic increase in production efficiency for the effective workers in plants with over 500 people in order to make up for the drastic increase in overhead (number of supportive employees.) Hence, increase in manufacturing efficiency barely keeps up with increase in administrative expenses.

TABLE 8-2

Total employees:	100	200	500	1000	2000	5000
Effective emlpoyees:	65	104	189	299	481	884
Supportive employees:	35	96	311	701	1519	4116
E/S ratio:	1.86	1.08	0.61	0.43	0.32	0.21

The above table also demonstrates quite vividly why smaller companies are able to compete successfully against industrial giants.

The question for the CEO is what category does his or her company fall under. One source for the answer is obviously the profit and loss statement. A low profit before earnings and taxes usually means a *bad* ratio between effective and supportive personnel. As a rule of thumb, if your operating profit before tax is 2% or less, you definitely have a low efficiency exponent. If profits are up to 10%, you probably fall into the Better category, and with profits exceeding 15%, you certainly are in the Optimum efficiency category. There may, of course, be extenuating circumstances that distort your profit picture such as a strike or a recession; therefore, it is best to use five-year averages. Another way to judge your firm is to divide the effective number into the total number of employees. Use 100 total and 65 effective as a basis,* then consult Table 8-1 and see where you stand.

For example: Your current total employment is 980 of which you classify 310 as effective. Now your total employment

---

* I consider 65 effective out of a total employment of 100 an optimal number for a manufacturing plant.

has increased from the baseline of 100 by 980/100 = 9.8 times, and the number of effective workers by 310/65 = 4.8 times using the "65" bench mark numbers from Table 8-2 (first column). Looking at Table 8-1, we find that in Group (A), the effective increase for a ten times increase in employment would have been 4.6. In Group (B), it is 5.6. So you fall somewhere in between with a ratio of 4.8.

The base figures of 100 for total and 65 for effective employees are somewhat arbitrary and would certainly vary by industry. If you run a multi-divisional enterprise, then you could use the smaller, or most efficient, division as a baseline in order to do a similar analysis.

The main point here is that as with living organisms, there is an inherent law that growth and efficiency of businesses cannot be scaled up at the same rate.

To keep growing and yet stay in Group (C) instead of Group (A) takes the talent of a superb manager. Simply increasing profit with increasing sales is not enough. Being able to increase profits *at the same rate* as sales is what truly separates a great manager from a mediocre one.

Returning back to business, here is an example of a valve and fitting business listed on the New York Stock Exchange and run by a very capable CEO. His growth record (mainly by acquisitions) is outstanding and showed an annual compounded growth rate of 16.6% over the past 15 years. Yet, his net profit grew only at a compounded rate of 14.5%! Since we may assume that profit is directly related to the ratio of effective to supportive personnel, then we may apply the *Law of the Sphere* just as well to the ratio between profit and sales volume, as long as the relationship between sales and number of effective workers remains constant.*

Let's examine the facts as stated in the company's annual report for 1997 and earlier years. In Figure 8-4, I have plotted net profit versus annual sales. As you can see, the number conforms well to the general trend given by the *Law of the Sphere* where, for example, 1997 profit = 1982 profit** x (Sales 1997/Sales 1982)$^{2/3}$. As the data clearly shows, while profit increases steadily, the *rate* of profit, i.e., the percentage of profit per given sales volume, keeps declining. I can well sympathize with this CEO's level of frustration. The percentage of profit keeps slipping despite his best efforts not realizing he is up against a natural law! And while his aim is to reach a sales volume of $1 billion before the second millenium (up from the present $720 million), he may only reach a net profit of 6.3% of sales as compared to the present 7.2% following the dictates of this law unless, of course, the IRS changes his tax bracket.

This example shows that in the absence of knowledge about the number of supportive and effective personnel, the sales to profit relationship may be used as an analytical tool using the *Law of the Sphere* to tell you, as a CEO, where your company is going.

---

* This, of course, implies that the number of supportive personnel
  increases exponentially in respect to sales volume, as it typically does.
** Increased to fit curve averages.

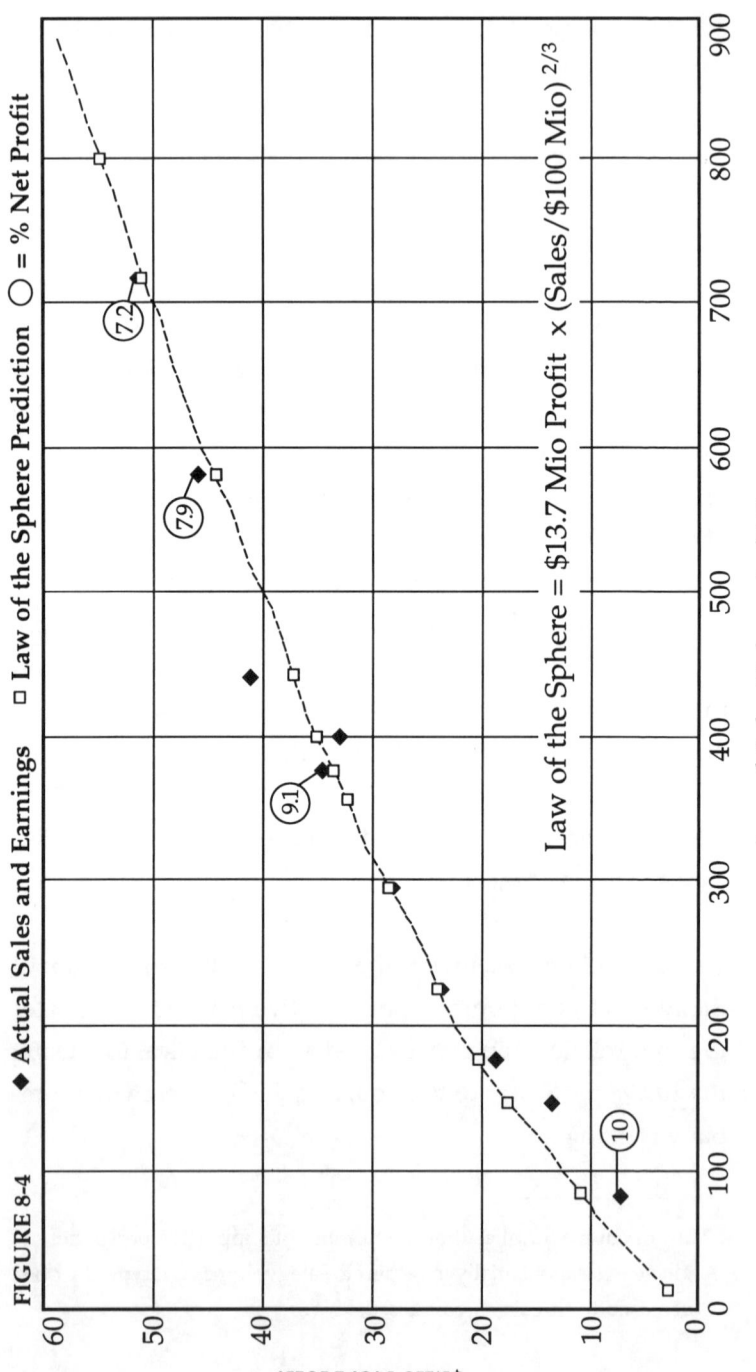

FIGURE 8-4

● Actual Sales and Earnings   □ Law of the Sphere Prediction   ○ = % Net Profit

Law of the Sphere = \$13.7 Mio Profit × (Sales/\$100 Mio)$^{2/3}$

Annual Sales Volume in \$Mio

\$Mio Net Profit

More to the point, this example clearly illustrates that company presidents should focus on profit not as an absolute number but as a percentage of sales volume. The CEO does an outstanding job only when the percentage of profit stays constant with increase in sales volume.

The chances are that unless "cloning" (see next sub chapter) or other steps are taken, there will be a decrease in the rate or percentage of profit when sales increase substantially as dictated by the *Law of the Sphere*, which redifined for this purpose states:

% profit = 100 x (profit at referenced sales volume/given sales volume) x (given sales volume/referenced sales volume)$^{2/3}$

Again using the data from figure 8-4 as an example, the percentage of profit for a future (given) sales volume of $1,000 Mio and using an actual past profit of $23 Mio shown for $220 Mio sales as reference is:
100 x ($23Mio/$1,000 Mio) x ($1,000 Mio/$220 Mio)$^{2/3}$= 6.3%

This mathematical relationship should be considered a major analytical tool for management in order to get a handle on plant efficiency. A higher percentage than the number calculated above with the aid of prior year's numbers* means you are very good. A lower percentage means there is a very serious problem and pruning may be in order.

---

* Prior sales and profit numbers should be corrected for inflation for enhanced accuracy.

Unfortunately, it is nearly impossible to find exact and published reports on the ratio between *effective* and *supportive* personnel. We do, however, find published data between profit (either as a total sum, or as a percentage of sales) and the employment figures of firms.

With few exceptions, the profit of a company is always low if the total employment is too high. In other words, companies employ too many people than are required to provide goods or services at competitive prices. Exceptions arise, for example, if the company rents expensive office space, or their business is based on importing hardware or material from a country whose currency value has increased substantially vis-a-vis the U.S. dollar. Nevertheless, these exceptions should not detract us from the overall relationship of the number of employees versus profit. Such a relationship can reflect the otherwise invisible ratio between *effective* and *supportive* personnel.

In my experience, it is very rare that the number of hours used to produce a certain part by an *effective* person varies between a small and a larger company. Such similarity, at least in the manufacturing sector, is already dictated by the use of machine tools, which are all run automatically and at optimum speed.

Hence, our conclusion has to be that the *only* reason why profit decreases in larger organizations is that the number of *supportive* personnel increases out of proportion to the necessary increase in the number of *effective* personnel. This

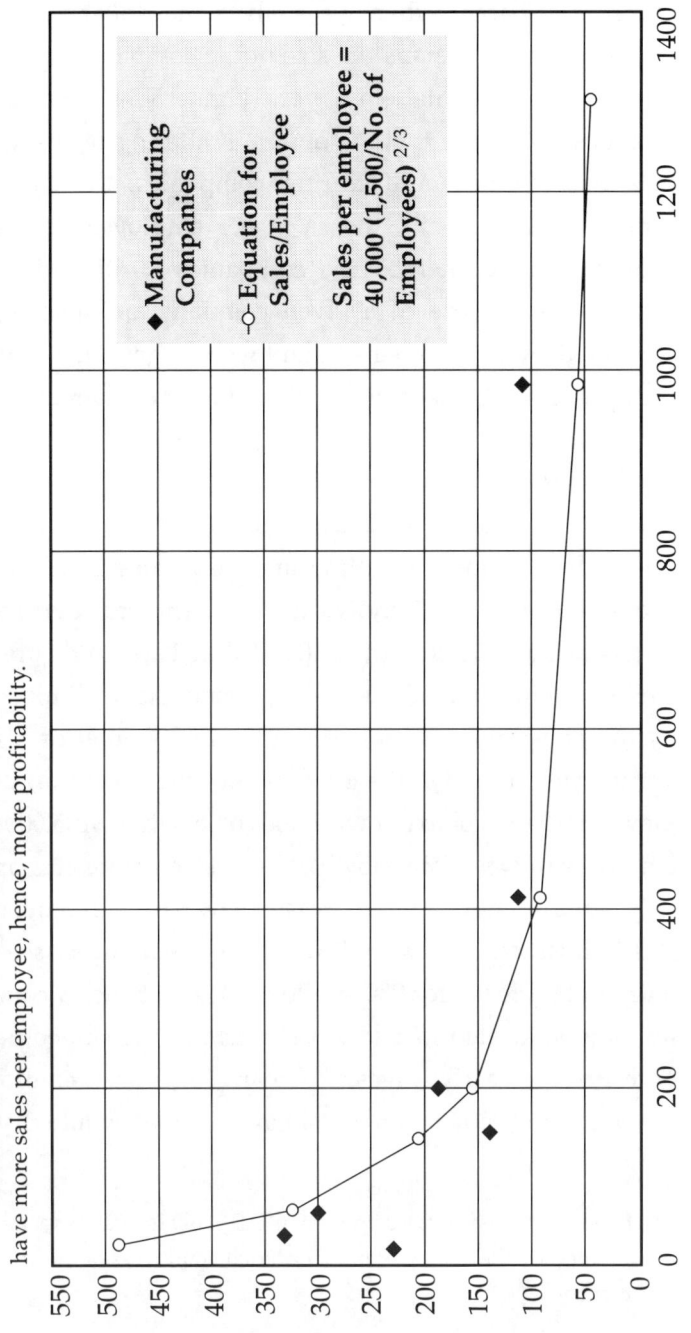

FIGURE 8-5 Relationship between sales per employee and total number of company employees. Small companies have more sales per employee, hence, more profitability.

Legend:
◆ Manufacturing Companies
–○– Equation for Sales/Employee

Sales per employee = $40{,}000 \, (1{,}500/\text{No. of Employees})^{2/3}$

X-axis: Number of Company Employees (0 to 1400)
Y-axis: Sales per Employee in $1,000 per Year (0 to 550)

becomes apparent when we analyze the dollar sales per person per year* versus the size of the company expressed in the number of total employees. Figure 8-5 shows such a relationship. While there is quite a scattering of the available data from manufacturing companies, the trend is unmistakable. Again, the sales per employee decreases drastically (and thereby the companies' profit) with the increase in the size of a given company, or division, as expressed by its number of employees. Again, the Law of the Sphere can be used as a tool to at least explain and predict this trend.

A WORD OF CAUTION: Exponential curves or equations cannot be extended ad infinitum. Reasonable benchmarks should be set for each individual case. The projected value of $386,000 per 50 employees (in 1997 dollars) in Figure 8-5 (solid line) may already be too high since such a limit is set by the physical capacity of an individual worker or his or her machine tool. On the other side of the spectrum, there may not be any company with sales of less than $105,000 per employee (lowest data shown). If it existed before, it is probably bankrupt now. Another reason why we have companies still in business with very low sales per employee (see the entry in Figure 8.5 for 980 employees) is that such a company may be located in a low wage area of the United Sates with average yearly wages of perhaps $25,000 per employee instead of $50,000 in high cost areas. This then would distort

---

* Defined as the yearly sales volume in U.S. Dollars of a company
    divided by the average number of total employees of the same
    company.

the statistics accordingly. This would mask an equivalent *high wage* sales per employee of only $50,000 due to the wage differential.

As in nature, nothing is exactly predictable. On the other hand, nothing in nature follows linear relationships and, as the graphs in this chapter clearly show, neither is the relationship linear between company size (number of employees) and profit. The reader may rightfully argue that the *Law of the Sphere* is not applicable in all cases, and he may be right. But even the most skeptical reader should admit that an exponential relationship does exist. If so, then the we only argue about the numerical value (or values) of the exponential factor in our equation.

Remember, all our effort in controlling human economic endeavor is really an attempt to control chaos, yet it is good to have some guidelines.

How to reverse the process

Any good manager having *inherited* a large company may ask him or herself the question: Can the process of exponential administrative growth be reversed? The answer is...probably not. One may consider splitting the company in two or three parts (if this is possible from the given product structure). This is a so-called *de-merger*, a ploy not so much exercised to gain efficiency (which it does not do, see explanation below), but to gamble that the stock market value of each of the individual new divisions combined will exceed the stock value of the old parent company.

Why does a de-merger not improve efficiency? Well, consider the *Law of the Sphere*. If you divide a large sphere (the parent company) into, say, two equal halves, you still get the same ratio between *effective* and total personnel (ratio between curved surface area and volume). For example, Company A has 10,000 employees. According to the 2/3rd *Law of the Sphere*, (see Table 8-1), there are about 2,200 effective employees (using 100 as base level) and 7,800 supportive employees, or a ratio of about 3.5 supportive to 1 effective. If you split this company *A* into two equal parts *B* and *C*, then each of *B* and *C* has 1,100 effective and 3,900 supportive personnel...still a ratio of 3.5 to 1!

In contrast, if *B* and *C* would have grown by itself from humble beginnings to a total of 5,000 employees each, they would have had 1,357 *effective* and 3,643 *supportive* personnel, or a ratio of only 2.68 to 1. This could have improved the productivity and, therefore, the profit before tax by [(1357 / 1100) x 100] - 100 = 23%. Alas, you can never start all over. So what are our choices?

Well, one way to keep growing efficiently while at the same time improving your bottom line is to grow sideways. What I mean by this is to buy one or more smaller competitors, preferably in the $50 million or below sales range (that is before they too become *water logged*.) The trick here is to maintain their independence. The temptation is usually too irresistible for the staff people of the larger parent company (the buyer) to impose their own *good will* onto the unfettered hierarchy of the smaller purchased company. Such impositions start from the most innocent requests for a *uniform financial reporting system* (with the resultant need for a brand new computer system) to environmental regulations, patent systems, *combined* purchasing efforts, prescribed engineering and drafting practices, to more hurtful pressures on inventory levels. All this is usually done behind the back of the CEO of the parent company, who is, most of the time, quite a common sense type of a person.

The requests are quite innocuous starting with a simple e-mail message from corporate headquarters. How long can the new General Manager (usually an up and coming executive from the parent company) refuse such a request? Usually not for very long, if he still wants to be considered a *team player*! This means interference from his own staff has to be strongly opposed by the parent company's CEO. This should be rule number one.

Rule number two is to limit the growth of the acquired company to a manageable level and then start a new practical company, typically by splitting up parts of the product lines of the original company. What you should do is clone, and upon growth, keep on cloning the well-run new division.

The following is an example of how a small, acquired company with, say, 100 people, of whom 60 are in the effective and 40 are in the supportive categories can grow. Assume further that the company has $25 million in yearly sales. Expenses are 32% labor, 20% material, and 20% other expenses. This leaves a profit before taxes of 28% or $7 million. Now let's look at two different approaches to growth.

Assume the acquiring corporation is well-run and falls in the *excellent* category where the number of effective personnel grows by a factor of 0.875 (modified spherical law), or $X = Y(B/A)^{7/8}$ where X is the number of effective employees and B is the total number of employees. Assume further that

TABLE 8-3

Company Size "B" (# of persons)[1]	Yearly Sales ($mio)[2]	No. of Eff. Personnel "X"	No. of Supp. Personnel	Total Wages[3] ($ mio)	Material & Other (40%)	Profit $ mio	Profit %
100	25	60	40	8	10	7	28
200	46	110	90	16	18.4	11.6	25
400	84	202	198	32	34	18	21
800	154	370	430	64	62	28	18
1600	282	679	921	128	113	41	15
3200	519	1245	1955	256	208	55	10
6400	951	2283	4117	512	380	59	6
12800	1745	4188	8612	1024	698	23	1.3

[1] Total employment
[2] $417,000 per effective personnel
[3] $80,000 per employee

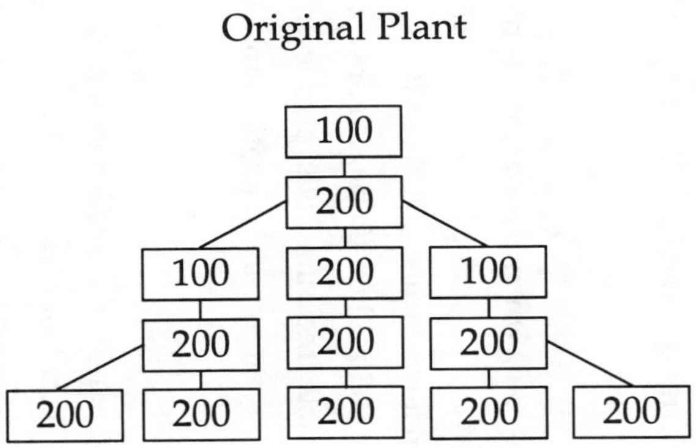

Total $ Sales	Profit $	% Profit	Total Eff. Employees	Total Employee
25	7	28	60	100
46	11.6	25	110	200
96	25.6	27	230	400
138	34.8	25	330	600
188	49	26	450	800

Original Plant

All sales and profit numbers are in $ millions.

Figure 8-6
How cloning a company can maintain high profitability while increasing sales volume. In this example, an initial plant with 100 employees evolves into five separate plants with a total of 800 employees.

the labor efficiency and the cost per employee ($80,000 per person) stay the same. The reference number A is 100 from above and the number of effective employees Y is 60; therefore, $X = 60 \, (B/100)^{7/8}$.

Keeping only one subsidiary, the growth scenario may look something like this using the above equation:

One can clearly see what happens here. Despite a great and well-run central management team (7/8 factor), the percent of profit degenerates steadily and there will be a loss once employment exceeds 13,500. Incidentally, using an exponential factor of 2/3 (the true sphere), the company would already be in the red at only 3,000 employees!

To contrast this, let's assume we will split up each subdivision once the employment figures exceed 200 (the *cloning* approach).

As you can see from Figure 8-6, when the overall employment reaches 800, you have five independent (or more) operating subdivisions with a total sales of $188 million and a pre-tax operating profit of $49 million (26%). Contrast this with the single company with the same 800 people from Table 8-2 having sales of $154 million and a profit before tax of only $28 million (18%)!

This may be an idealized case, not all cloned divisions grow at the same rate for example. Nevertheless, it serves as a guide on how to approach the problem of finding a way to stay efficient while growing. The ultimate success of this approach depends on grooming good general managers who are adept at understanding the philosophy of staying *lean* and who are willing to maintain the proven management organization and style of the originally cloned successful division.

Chapter 8

How the Government Can Help You

Government legislated assistance is the only help
a businessperson is forced to accept.

The above title sounds like an oxymoron and in some cases
it is since the endless stream of mostly federal government
regulations, but eagerly copied on the state and even local
goverment* levels, can stifle private enterprise, or at least
make it very expensive to conduct business.

All government regulations or census requests start (as do
some wars nowadays) from very noble intentions. The basic

---

* There are now about 80,000 separate governmental entities in the
 United States according to Alex N. Pattakos as stated in
 "Rediscovering the Soul of Business," *New Leader Press*, Sterling
 Stone, Inc., San Francisco, CA, 1995.

and most common reason for the issuance of a new regulation is to *aid* business. Another reason is to help or protect the workers. Additional regulations are intended, for example, to help collect taxes or duties.

Some of those regulations, usually the outgrowth of some legislation passed by congress or state houses, have sound reasoning and actually contribute to the well being of workers or the economy. Others are not, and can be a gross distortion of the original legislative intent. In any case, there is typically no accounting of what the law or regulation would do in terms of the cost impact on private businesses or the national economy. For example, if one would add up the number of parking spaces for the handicapped and compare it to the actual number of handicapped people in our nation that are able to drive or be driven, the number would startle you. If it would not be politically incorrect, such a study could be the worthy subject of a $50 million federal grant. I am sure you have cruised through a full parking lot at a local shopping mall and spotted the dozens of empty *reserved for handicapped* spaces.

Speaking of federal help, there are clever business persons able to take advantage of the seemingly unending federal ways to financially aid *deserving* businesses beginning with low cost loans from the Small Business Administration to outright grants (sometimes the result of special effort by the local Senator or Congressman). The problem is that these funds are available only for business owners (or prospective business owners) with access to well-connected law offices who specialize, for a generous fee (which may take the larger portion of the resultant grant) in filling out the required hundreds of pages of supporting documentation for such a grant.

What sometimes makes government laws and regulations so fiendish is the fact that the mere publication of a new regulation in the Federal Register instantly makes you a potential subject for punishment for non-compliance. The simple fact that no human being is able to read the thousands of pages of the Federal Register, which is printed daily, let alone understand their meaning and remember them, is no legal excuse when you are in front of the judge should you get caught for non-compliance.

True to the *Law of the Sphere*, larger countries (like larger companies) have bigger governments, which absorb a larger share of the country's gross national product than a smaller country. A smaller country's or state's bureaucracy intervenes less because it simply does not have a large enough staff to draft more regulations.*

From a business perspective, we can subdivide laws and regulations into those that are benign (such as fixing the dates of national holidays) and others that can seriously affect our business in the following ways:

1. Absorb extra manhours for awareness or compliance purposes.
2. Require additional operating capital.
3. Mandate extra manufacturing space and building

---

* "Little Countries," *The Economist*, January 3, 1998, pp. 67.

alterations.

4. Force you to redesign or, worse, obsolete your products.

5. Require a usually more costly, revised method of manufacturing.

The main, albeit unintended, negative side effect of governmental regulations is the potential for the demise of small entrepreneurial companies, which unlike larger, well-capitalized competitors don't have the financial or manpower resources to comply with the regulations. To explain, it is easy for a 2000 employee company to employ an OSHA specialist and somebody who handles all environmental problems, but quite another matter for a smaller company employing only 20 people. The large company only adds 0.1% to the payroll (2 people out of 2000) while the small company adds 10%! Yet, for all practical purposes, both have to comply with the same regulations.

The effect of this unproportionally high burden imposed on small entrepreneurs is restricting their growth on which much of our country's wealth depends. Not only do small companies provide new ideas for products and services but small and mid-size companies hire more new employees than do large, established enterprises.

A word about census requirements. You may be familiar with the sometimes ten pages of forms that appear in the mail from either the federal or state government with some city forms thrown in. All these forms demonstrate a noble purpose such as spotting economic trends in your business or documenting the employment figures in your community, for example. I suspect another, unstated motive. If it takes five workers in a given agency to evaluate one page of a questionnaire, then it will take at least 25 workers to evaluate five pages. This not only creates job security at this particular agency, but also is a reason for a legitimate request to increase the agency's budget (adding one page requires five more people!). Of course, any questionnaire is not complete without the extra piece of paper that explains the *paper saving act.*

A friend of mine handled this matter in his own, down to earth way. He first looked at the fine print at the bottom of the form. If it did not say *failure to comply with this request is punishable by a fine of up to $10,000 for the first offense, etc.,"* then he simply deep-sixed the forms in his waste backet. Unfortunately, more and more government agencies heard about my friend who fiendishly tried to deprive agency workers to earn their livelihood. Consequently, they persuaded a compliant congress to add the aforementioned penalty clause to most forms. Well, sometimes you can't win.

As a owner or manager of a small business, you should handle governmental regulations as follows:

1. Read a lot to keep yourself informed.
2. Send your entire payroll through an outside firm that specializes in handling your paychecks and all related federal, state, and city forms for a nominal fee.
3. Ask your insurance carrier to fill you in on the latest OSHA requirements.

4. Hire a good consultant or attorney if you are faced with a problem.

5. Read publications published by your trade association.

6. File your old census forms or state questionnaires in a safe place. You will save a lot of time by copying most of the old information the next time around.

7. Don't buy real estate for your new plant without a thorough investigation of the environment (soil, water). When in doubt, lease the land and buildings.

8. Scared of wrongful discharge or sexual harassment suits? Hire as many temporary workers as possible. At least this will give you a first line of defense. (I have known of a company that had the same *temporary* employee for over 30 years!)

Of course, if I had been Mr. Thomas Jefferson, or one of his friends, I would have added to the Constitution of the United States that "no new law or regulation could be passed without simultaneously eliminating an existing one."

Chapter 9

How to Manage a Company, or How Not to Follow The Old Rules

The purpose of a business is to make money,
not to make or sell widgets.

Having been employed for 23 years at small- and mid-sized corporations both in the United States and Europe, prior to forming my own company, allowed me the luxury of observing, first hand, the many mistakes made by management. These mistakes reduced profits and squandered valuable monetary resources. Perhaps even worse, sometimes bad decisions also led to morale problems with the employees, most of who were quite capable in detecting and observing unsound decisions.

Why do many managers seemingly make irrational decisions?

In my opinion, the reasons are in part because:

1. A manager was promoted to a position which he is not capable of filling. This is the so-called *Peter's Principle*.

2. Frequently managers do not understand basic business principles on how to generate profit. In other words, they are not trained to think like entrepreneurs.

3. Related to the above, most managers, even CEOs graduated through lower positions with a tendency to adhere to unwritten company rules (*don't rock the boat!*).

4. Managers are very security conscious. Unfortunately, not conscious of their company's security, but of their own. This stifles initiative.

5. Often managers and CEOs blindly follow the latest trend or fad in their given field of business. It may be ISO 9000, or the latest software packages, without regard to cost-benefits. (However, they appear to be modern in the eyes of their peers!).

6. Many managers are incapable of understanding technical or intricate financial problems in their department and, therefore, have to rely on the advice of their staff. This leads to *blind* decision-making. The manager was promoted into his or her position through *seniority* or *connections* rather than expertise in a given field.

Besides the apparent ineptitude of some of my former managers, I also learned that many unsound company decisions were based on bad marketing, or worse, to satisfy some obscure internal financial habits.

A case in point: A mid-size corporation I worked for some years ago purchased a smaller valve manufacturing company founded twenty years earlier by a clever engineer. In order to reduce his investment, he decided to forego the purchase of expensive machine tools and instead subcontracted the machining of all parts. This left, besides administrative personnel, only a few assembly workers. The results were a consistent 25% to 28% profit before tax—a fact that made the takeover attractive to the buyer when the owner decided to retire.

After the formal takeover of this well-run company by my employer, the accountants were in for a shock; there were not enough direct hours to absorb the overhead burden! In other words, the Accounting Department of the purchasing company was unable to do proper cost accounting under their own well-established rules for the products made by the acquired firm.

This created quite a panic within top management. After some frantic meetings, it was decided to purchase machine tools for several million dollars and hire the requisite number of machinists (more *direct* labor). This satisfied the accountants, but caused havoc with the efficiency of this smaller, purchased plant. Its profits within the first year after being purchased dropped by 60%!

I never forgot this valuable lesson, and my first action after forming my own firm was to find outside vendors to do the machining of my parts. *This should be Rule No. 1!* Besides the obvious savings in capital and floor space, there are other not so obvious advantages. One is the saving in labor with the associated headaches of personnel problems, training, pensions, etc. Another advantage of great importance is the absolute predictability of product cost. The total cost of a finished item is simply the sum of the listed invoiced amounts for the individual parts. You simply don't pay the invoice if a part is machined wrong (formerly you had to absorb the cost as overhead in your own machine shop). Incidentally, this works wonders for your Quality Control Department too.

Aside from assembly time, which is pretty constant, there are very few variable cost items which makes it possible to have a very accurate profit and cost statement at the end of each month.

Rule No. 2 is to try to avoid having a Human Resource or Payroll Dept. Related to the above is the effort to have as few employees as possible. (This includes part-time or outsourced employees—a ruse used by many managers to bypass strict no-hire policies!) The result, besides the obvious increase in profit, is no need for a Human Resource and Payroll Department, at least for companies with fewer than 100 employees. All payroll work can be out-sourced to data processing companies who, for a few dollars per employee, can also keep track of the never-ending Federal and State rules and regulations besides filing timely payroll tax returns for your company. Screening new employees can be done by employment agencies. I encourage you to hire temporary help (but not for the purpose of showing a low payroll on your monthly profit and loss report). If they work out, you can always hire them later. If they don't fit, then all it takes is a phone call to terminate their employment without any messy legal entanglements.

Rule No. 3 is do not use a Purchasing Department. The next *not to have* on my list is a Purchasing Department. While still young, I observed that a purchasing agent does not know what to purchase. He or she relies instead on written requisitions from other departments who specify quantity and, usually, vendor sources. This convinced me that re-typing a requisition is a very non-essential activity.

So instead of a person in the factory writing a requisition for a given material, he simply generates the purchase order himself. This not only saves personnel, but also time (delivery time is the key to a customer's happiness). Well, you may ask, how about the skill of a good purchasing agent to negotiate prices, or to avoid conflict of interest or bribes? These are mostly myths. I cannot recall having met a Purchasing Manager who understood the technical requirements, the quality aspects, and delivery needs, as well as the person who needs the part of the equipment. Besides, the initial vendor selection should always be based on multiple price quotation. Otherwise, the up to 20% margin on top of the parts prices to cover the cost of a Purchasing Department saved makes up for some improprieties (should it happen).

Rule No. 4 is don't split lines of responsibility. What I mean by that is to make sure vital functions are controlled by a single manager who assumes responsibility. For example, if you have a Plant Manager who is responsible for producing and shipping out goods to your customers on time, make sure he has complete control of procurement for parts and material. If you don't, then you have to listen to endless complaints and excuses why an order was delayed. The Production Manager will blame the Purchasing or Planning Manager for not getting material or parts, and the latter will complain for not getting a timely requisition or sales forecast. You will begin to pull your hair out!

Another obsession with efficiency of modern management is inventory turn over (ITO). This is driven by financial consideration....a low inventory means more cash is available for investment. This sounds good in theory, but not always a profitable way to do business.

In my company, the turnover ratio was a measly 2.5; that is, a given part stayed on the shelf for about five months. This is, of course, an average figure. Some parts stayed less than three months, others for eight or nine months. The reasons were two-fold: First, instead of buying smaller quantities of goods many times, we purchased larger quantities typically four times a year. This gave us substantially lower costs from our vendors (less set up time). Secondly, by keeping a *high* inventory, we virtually never ran out of parts. What this meant was that we could fulfill 90% plus of all customers orders in a matter of hours and at a hefty premium!

Here is a little math to show you how this "disrespect" for ITO paid off. Assume you have a $10 million inventory when the ITO is 2.5, and an inventory of $6.25 million with an ITO of 4. The capital outlay to carry it 4.8 months (ITO = 2.5) instead of the desired 3 months (ITO = 4) at say 9% bank

interest. The extra interest cost per year is
$$(\$10,000,000 - \$6,250,000) \times .09$$
$$\text{or } \$337,500.$$

Suppose with an inventory turnover of 2.5 ($10 million in stock) we can ship 10% of all goods on an expedited delivery schedule (because we have parts on hand) and assuming further that the average sales price is 2.6 times inventory cost. The extra profit earned based on a 15% *quick ship* add on is:
$$0.10 \times 2.5 \times 2.6 \times \$10,000,000 \times 0.15$$
$$\text{or } \$975,000$$

That is a 260% return on money wasted in inventory! To that, you have to add up to $6.5 million of extra sales volume because your competitors cannot match your delivery schedule. One has to realize that this inventory leverage disappears quickly with a decrease in gross profit. For example, if the gross profit had only been 35% instead of the assumed 61.5%, then the return on quick ship sales would have only been $576,932 instead of $975,000.

Since my former company's gross profit averaged 68%, i.e., the inventory (cost of parts) was only 32% of the average sales price, we effectively turned the inventory over an impressive 7.8 times when compared to the sales volume (yearly sales volume divided by the value of inventory). This compares to only about 6 times inventory on sales volume by my larger competitors. Let's call this *Rule No. 5*.

It turned out that I was not alone in this philosophy. The

New Hampshire based Cabletron Corporation with over $1 billion in yearly sales had an ITO of less than 3 but a turnover of sales to inventory of close to 8:1! Need I say that Cabletron had profits of about 35% before tax? Not surprisingly, their business philosophy was identical to ours.... Keep as much inventory on hand to sell every product off-the-shelf. This was the key to their phenomenal growth rate compared to their competitors who followed rigid accounting rules.

Rule No. 6 concerns how you train your employees. As rightly pointed out by Hammer and Champy* modern workers, especially in non-factory occupations, should be trained to be *generalists* instead of *specialists*. That is, employees should be trained to perform several tasks. This, almost by default, requires they be given freedom to make decisions. It is probably less harmful for a company to allow employees to make occasional mistakes than to establish a too ridged hierarchical management system.

A case in point: Internal sales people in my former company performed multiple functions starting with such mundane tasks as answering the telephone and entering customer orders into the computer to advising customers on technical problems (with backup from engineering if required), to selling to customers and writing million dollar quotations. This was all in a days work and it created not only a lively work day (no boredom here), but a kindred spirit of comradeship.

---

* Hammer and Champy, Reengineering the Corporation, (New York: Harper Business, 1993)

In another company I happened to know quite well, the Sales Department was rigidly departmentalized. First, the telephone is routed through an operator and through the infamous *voice mail*. Second, the sales people were forbidden to talk directly to customers (all customer requests were to be referred to the local sales representative). Third, there was to be no more direct sales effort by company people. Fourth, all internal sales staff was subdivided into geographical areas of responsibility, each handling only an assigned number of representative firms. The invariable result was that employee *A* had his phone mail overloaded while employee *B* in the *cubicle* next to him (yes, everybody had the made famous *Dilbert* cubicle space!) went for a walk through the shop out of sheer boredom.

Rule No. 7 is don't use organizational charts. This sounds like a strange request, but it need not be. Along with titles, organization charts tend to *lock* managers into specific duties rather than utilizing their talents over a wide a spectrum as possible. Don't worry, an employee will always know who his or her boss is even without a title or slot on the organization chart. I ran my multi-million dollar company for 18 years without ever needing a chart. But I had to invent one in a hurry to satisfy the buyer of my company during Due Diligence.

Rule No. 8, do away with headquarter staff. Larger corporations should do away with their headquarter staff departments such as Legal, Finance, Environmental, Human Resources, etc. Those are like cancerous growth in an organism. Not only do they have to be paid for by *allocations of corporate expenses* to be paid for by individual divisions, but they, like government bureaucracy, want to extend their power and influence by telling you how to organize your cost system, how to interview personnel, send you endless safety advice, and so on. All this is done with the very best of intentions. The trouble is certain rules that may apply to a 800,000 square foot plant may not apply to one at 30,000 square feet. This *benevolent burden* hits especially smaller subsidiaries or plants. An *Environmental Manager* in a larger plant has time to interact with the respective corporate vice president and his or staff, but with a smaller plant, the burden falls perhaps on the Plant Manager who is kept from making sure the shipping schedule is filled for the month. Instead, he is commanded to an urgent meeting 1,000 miles away to discuss the impact of the latest Federal Regulations.

Mr. Koch, President of the Koch Company, one of the largest privately held U.S. corporations, has the right idea. Let your corporate staff compete on the open market. Instead of simply imposing a forced fee (allocations) onto your division, let each division contact a local attorney (if, for example, there is a legal problem) *and the* corporate legal staff. Find out which is less expensive and proceed accordingly. Mr. Koch apparently knows what he is doing. Too bad he does not publish his profit statements. I suspect it is quite good.

For following the above rules, you and your company may be rewarded with something resembling the following financial results, which reflect my own company's balance sheet the year prior to the sales of its assets:

Yearly sales volume per company employee:*	$331,000
Net profit before taxes as percent of sales:	29%
Return on original capital invested before tax:	290% per year
Return on working capital before tax:	52%

And remember, "Profit is the only form of praise for a job well done which cannot be bought."

One final bit of advice. No matter how much you are tempted, try not to be the first to buy a new device, equipment, or tooling even if it is highly recommended. The reason is simple....any new technology needs time to mature, i.e., to eliminate the initial design defects and other shortcomings. In addition, first production runs tend to be rather expensive (the initial tooling and R&D expenses have to be absorbed). Therefore, the wise counsel is to be patient and wait until your competitors have tried it. While competitors may get more advertising mileage for being *technically up-to-date*, (or for being cool), they are also saddled with training their employees, higher maintenance expenses, unexpected breakdowns, and other unpleasantness directly affecting their bottom line.

A case in point is numerically controlled machine tools.

---

* Price adjusted for 1997. Incidentally, I consider this figure my most important management tool even though nobody else thinks of it.

When they came on the scene in about 1972, they were of limited use, had primitive electronics prone to breakdowns, and were hard to program. Yet, few manufacturers wanted to be left out of having at least one, lest they be accused of being old-fashioned.

When one of my friends (the president of a larger manufacturing firm) asked me what he should do, I counseled patience. Sure enough, within four to five years numerically controlled machine tools became a well working and, today, an indispensable tool of modern production. By waiting, my friend bought himself well-working products while saving himself all the expensive headaches of the earlier users.

Chapter 10

Rules For Successful Management

1. Manage your business to make profit and not to manufacture or sell widgets.

2. Try to have only three layers of management.

3. Become, and stay, the master of your computer systems.

4. Design your computer software program to enter, produce, and ship customer orders, and *not* to satisfy the Accounting Department.

5. Don't do or buy things because they are nice or fashionable. Purchase only what is absolutely necessary! This is especially true for your computer/information system where the *Fad de Jour* can be extremely expensive.

6. Solve problems immediately. They cost you twice as much

after one week and four times as much after one month, at which time you've lost a customer.

7. Do not manage by committee. Most successful managers are benevolent dictators.

8. Keep your lines of communication short and avoid meetings like the plague.

9. The most efficient company is a small company (see *Law of the Sphere*). If you have to grow, then subdivide.

10. Do not ask your subordinates to do things you would not be able or willing to do yourself.

11. A well run department can do all the required work within eight hours a day!

12. Do not create departments whose work can be done elsewhere, and assign managers to non-profit contributing departments on a temporary basis only.

13. Don't fall for fads such as ISO 9000. They can be very expensive. (However, encourage your competitors to do so!)

14. If there are any questions left, don't go to outside consultants, use your common sense.

15. Train your managers so they are able to run their departments without any external guidance, including your own.

16. Have a *real* person greet your customers when they call your company and outlaw all voice mail (except, perhaps, for interoffice use).

Chapter 11

CHASING THE RAINBOW OR
HOW TO GET STARTED

Never confuse market research with wishful thinking.

Ever wondered about the lack of new technological developments? No, I am not talking about the latest improved software programs.

Consider jet planes for a minute. Their basic design was completed during World War II. What we see now is larger or faster versions of it. Consider television or tape recorders, which were both developed 50 to 60 years ago. We keep improving the designs such as using microprocessors instead of the vacuum tube, which gave us the chance to miniaturize electronic equipment and to run it faster, but it did not create any new basic technologies. Nothing yet has replaced the automobile as our principle mode of transportation. Rocket technology was developed in the 1920s and 1930s. Their size has increased and guidance systems have been improved, but that is all.

Our common household appliances date back more than 80 years. Sure we have more bells and whistles on a dryer but that does not improve the basic method of drying our laundry! Radar was developed in the 1930s and so on.

There are, of course, exceptions. For example, the more recent development of laser technology created a host of new products and enables us to use laser disk technology to vastly improve data storage and retrieval. But compared to the period between 1930 and 1950, the progress is puny indeed.

Maybe it is a moot point to ask such questions about the lack of progress, but I don't think so! The absence of developments of new technologies reflects a basic cultural change in our society. This is not only restricted to the lack of progress in sciences and technologies, but is also apparent in the lack of cultural achievements such as the lack of outstanding writers (where is today's Steinbeck, Faulkner, or Hemingway?); great composers (No, I don't count the Grateful Dead!); and great painters (where are they?).

It is perhaps up to the philosophers to speculate on the origins of such a cultural malaise (which, on the other side of the coin, creates negative effects such as a high crime rate, higher teenage suicide rates, and drug problems).

The explanation I prefer is: This is the result of a lack of challenge and, therefore, a lack of purpose. The first one is an undesirable by-product of our high standard of living. For the overwhelming majority of Americans, all the basic needs for food, clothing, and housing are fulfilled. Our most pressing problem seems to be deciding which is the most exciting new movie to go to and see.

Gone are the great depression days, a very good motivator indeed for our grandparents, and World War II and the Korean War for our parents. It is astounding to read the suicide statistics in times of war or famine, which are virtually zero! Back then we were too busy trying to survive so we had neither the time nor inclination to kill ourselves.

The particular cultural malaise I am talking about is not a new phenomenon. For example, it occurred before in China during the middle of the second millennia, which was caused primarily by the teachings of Taoism as espoused by Lieh-Tzu in about 400 A.D. In the 18th century, the government under Tai Cheng more or less mandated the *do not question the laws of nature* philosophy making research and development socially unacceptable. It also occurred in Europe after the fall of the Roman Empire starting around 400 AD and lasting until the beginning of the Renaissance.

The way I see it, this cultural/technological malaise is the major cause of Japan's economic slump over the past ten years. We may blame this on the decrease in real estate prices or the Japanese bank crisis, but these are only the effects of the underlying technological crisis...not the cause.

For the past 50 years, Japan has managed to exploit inventions made either in the United States or in Europe and very skillfully convert them into efficient and mostly low-cost consumer products. This strategy works as long as there are new basic innovations waiting to be exploited. However, within the last 10 to 15 years, this particular well has dried up. There indeed may be a limit of how many improvements you can make on a camcorder or a CD player.

What is worse, is that the lesser-developed Asian countries now manufacture much of the same products which Japan manufactures, albeit at lower labor rates! This is a serious problem not only for Japan, but also for the western countries since we are so financially and economically intertwined.

The cure would be for the U.S. (and Europe) to again develop new, basic technologies such as the means to supplant the automobile or develop entertainment devices that gratify not only the eye and ear (as is done presently), but also the sense of smell and touch. Alas, inventions cannot be commanded by government grants nor by the monetary largess of a corporation. They mostly derive from the vision and hard work of individuals (much the same as artists do their works). Unfortunately, there are now cultural roadblocks (as there were in Asia), which tend to prevent this from happening: (1) the lack of motivation (no empty stomach!); (2) the lack of education (consider the ratio of engineers to attorneys in the United States!); and, finally, (3) the fallacy of corporate policies to insist on doing research and development (meaning *inventing*) by teams only.

Pardon me for digressing. You may rightly ask, what has this got to do with me becoming an entrepreneur interested in starting my own business? You may not realize this, but it has a lot to do with it. Since we cannot all be a Bill Gates, we have to be realistic. The lack of new technologies also prevents you from exploiting new markets for new gadgets that the public would be eager to buy, thereby, opening up new profit opportunities. Instead, like the majority of all businesses, you are forced to manufacture or sell *me too* products, i.e., second-hand technology.

Now, you can do this four ways:

1. Purchase and use new and superior manufacturing techniques, thereby lowering costs and out-selling your competitor. This possibility is somewhat remote. The chances are your competitor, who is himself under price pressure, has thought of this already.

2. Reduce the quality of a product by using less expensive materials and/or fewer parts thereby cutting costs. Not very ethical, but a widely practiced art in making a buck, or

3. If you are technically inclined, you can always redesign and improve the performance of an old technology. Consider how many times Sony Corp. has redesigned the good old tape recorder, each time with astonishing financial success. Redesigning and improving on old core technologies keeps 90% of all businesses going!

Mr. R.H. Jenrette* was only half right when he stated that when consultants say, *"return to your old core business,"* corporate rigor mortis sets in. There are indeed still many ways to modify and live off such improved core business products that will keep you from going under!

4. Run a more efficient enterprise. Make a profit in a competitive environment by reducing overhead. If you have read the previous chapters, you already know how to do this.

However, before you decide to quit your job and become a budding capitalist, do your homework. Make a thorough marketing plan. Pick the product, study your competitors, and know their cost structure. Most importantly, know their weaknesses whether it is cost, quality, performance, or delivery. Exploiting such weaknesses will get you started. Keep in mind that *wishful thinking is no substitute for a realistic marketing or product plan.*

Try to manufacture only a few, "standardized" product lines. By "standard" I mean products that have the least amount of variation in design or material, leading to the possibility of mass producing the products. Resist the call by your sales force to add "bells and whistles" to your standard products. While this may bring your representative a few more sales and, therefore, commissions, your bottom line

---

* Richard H. Jenrette, Jenrette's *The Contrarian Manager*, (New York: McGraw-Hill, 1997).

will suffer. The resultant "specials" will need special attention not only in order entry, but also in Engineering, Planning, Procurement, and Assembly. There is additional cost that typically is not accounted for and which invariably affects the bottom line. When listening to the pleas of your representatives, keep this in mind: his commission is the same whether or not you make a profit. There is a common goal between the manufacturer and its sales force; that is, to increase the sales volume. However, when it comes to making a profit, motives are diametrically opposed! Do not forget this at your peril!

There certainly are niche businesses that specialize in producing specialty products. With proper organization, these businesses can be profitable. However, never ever combine the two, i.e., try to manufacturer "standard" and "special" products under the same roof.

Next, make a very conservative financial forecast keeping in mind that there will not be one dime of profit coming in for at least one year (not counting several months of hard work before your company even starts). Don't rely on banks for financing. You probably don't have enough collateral (if you had it, you would not need the loan). The best starting capital is your own savings. The emotional attachment to your *own* money will keep you from buying an expensive company car, fancy furniture, or elaborate computer equipment. Second hand items will do quite well until the money starts flowing in. Here is your choice: do you want to have a positive cash flow, or do you want to impress your friends and neighbors?

Also important is who you hire to support your enterprise. Cultivating good initial employees should start way before you get incorporated. These should be very talented and outstanding people. Knowing and observing them for many years will reveal their strengths and weaknesses. Remember, these initial employees will be your department managers when you start growing. For example, I have known the person who later became my vice president of sales for almost 20 years (when he still was a student) prior to engaging him. He was an excellent salesman but had a disdain for paperwork (as most good sales people do). This prevented him from getting promoted by his former employer into a managerial position, which, in turn, was lucky for me. Because he was not a good bureaucrat did not bother me. His sales ability was what counted. I simply put him in charge of an office manager who took care of the administrative details.

This brings up an important point. Most U.S. corporations over-emphasize administrative capabilities in their managers. For example, I know an air conditioner manufacturer* where the vice president of sales never sold an air conditioner; the vice president of technology never designed an air conditioner; the vice president of marketing sold farm machinery in his former job, and the vice president of manufacturing did not know the price of a pound of steel. Such management policies are a recipe for disaster! The CEO has to rely on all these managers to make the decisions that affect the future of his or her company. In order to do this,

---

* An assumed product to protect the innocent.

each manager, in turn, has to rely on the knowledge and good will of his or her subordinates. Good will is especially important since if this particular manager is not well liked (quite common in this situation since a superior with a lack of technical knowledge is likely to develop an inferiority complex that manifests itself by rude behavior towards underlings), he will be mislead on purpose. The corporate staff, who may be well versed in preparing earnings forecasts, are much like a group of blind people trying to cross a busy street with the aid of guide dogs when it comes to deciding how to counter a competitive threat or how to pick a product that will keep the company from going under.

Leadership Qualifications

The moment you hire employees or you become a head of a department, you in effect become a leader. What kind of a leader do you want to be? Unquestionably, all of us want to be loved, respected, and admired. The reality is quite different. Your group of employees or subordinates are quite a different bunch of people with diverse backgrounds and temperaments. Your carefully thought-out motivational strategy may work quite well with one or two persons, but may cause resentment or, worse, ridicule with others. This then calls for flexibility in your approach, and you have to take the time to study each person's personality. Never underestimate the intelligence of the people who work for you!

From my own, and admittedly very limited survey, here are the three most important characteristics that a boss should possess:

1. Honesty. This almost always comes first and covers such diverse matters as not being truthful about the financial conditions of the company, or pending layoffs (if you don't want to reveal such facts, say so, but don't fib), to promising raises or promotions, and then not following up and, even worse, stealing your subordinate's ideas.

2. Be receptive to your employees' or subordinates' ideas or suggestions. This sometimes is hard to do since the idea may not always be practical or cost effective. Try to be open and make an honest effort to evaluate each case. If your decision is positive, then reward the person. If negative, take time from your busy schedule and explain the reasons.

3. Fairness. This covers a lot of ground and may quite often be perceived differently between several people. For example, a promotion is considered a fair and deserved action by the person receiving the promotion, but invariably may be resented as unfair by another employee. It extends to the way pay raises or work assignments are handed out, to how your bonus plan is structured.

One thing you should not forget in judging the attitude of your people is that at least 90% of them think they are perfectly qualified to take over your job and able to do it better than you. This leads us to what I consider a very important qualification of any boss: be capable of understanding and even performing any job or task that your subordinate is capable of doing. This way you can teach them to do their job better, and it will enable you to help them out if they run into difficulties.

If you can do this, you will earn their respect.... a much more valuable and effective trait over the long run than the elusive *being loved*.

The most important qualification you should have as an *effective* boss is to have a great memory. Let me explain. You have to be able to remember each suggestion or command you give during the day (probably to many people) and then check later to see if it has been done. The reason is simple. Many subordinates may not like your plan or command; therefore, they tend to *forget about it*. If you forget too, then they win the argument the quiet way. You lose, and nothing gets done. On the other hand, if you remember and bring the subject up again, they feel exposed and will think twice before trying to circumvent your orders again.

One thing you have to realize is that starting a company is lots of things, but most of all is extremely hard work. This requires stamina to work 60 hours plus a week and is not something you want to undertake if you are over 50 years old. You also have to be prepared to give up your hobbies, such as playing golf. And perhaps, worst of all, be prepared to spend less time with your family. All this has to be discussed thoroughly with your family prior to making this move. They are the ones that will suffer, at least during the first few years.

Of course, having a partner does help. First, you can split the initial investment and the high workload. Secondly, you have a confident (and not a disinterested employee) to share your problems and concerns with. It will help and be even better if the partner is your spouse or close friend and who has suitable skills such as in accounting or personnel, for example. Handling the financial side is especially handy since this is an area where confidentiality and discretion are important.

However, before you start any undertaking with a partner, you better prepare an ironclad partnership agreement. A joint business venture is like a marriage; it can be a happy one and last forever, or it can end in a nasty divorce. You would be amazed to know how many taxi drivers I have met who claim they were cheated out of their businesses by a crooked partner. This brings up the next subject:

Legal Entanglements

I am not an attorney and having never been admitted to any bar, I should not tell you how to write agreements, even though you may be perfectly able and legally authorized to do so. Regardless of whether you or your attorney writes the contract, remember, the most important paragraph is the *escape clause*. In any good contract, there should be a specified way to terminate any contract without causing you or your partner irreparable harm. You should insist on this!

As long as there are attorneys, there will always be the chance that you may lose your business even without any fault of your own. You may be late with your loan payments, due to delays in customer payments, and the bank may want to repossess. Some disgruntled employee may sue you, or one of your products may have been installed in a factory that burned down and someone got hurt. The fact that your product had nothing to do with the fire is, unfortunately, no consideration when you are subpoenaed. It will cost you perhaps hundreds of thousands of dollars in legal fees to prove your innocence.

You may not have all that money to prove your innocence, especially when you are just starting out. You may also not have found an insurance company willing to write a product liability policy for an unknown company. So you may have to be prepared to fold your business before it really got started.

A friend of mine devised a special way to solve this dilemma. He arranged his company's finances in such a manner that the net assets were never more than a token sum. In other words, he withdrew any unneeded cash by paying dividends or distributions to his partners and then, in turn, put up outside loans (sometimes from the same partners) to balance whatever equity there was in business property or inventory. His thinking was that no attorney worth his salt would bother to sue a company whose net worth was zero. There wouldn't even be enough assets to pay his legal fees. I think my friend probably had something there.

How Much Starting Capital Do I Need?

The important thing is to keep your starting capital as low as possible. There are three reasons: (1) there is less money to borrow or save, (2) with less capital invested, any profit will provide you with a higher rate of return on your capital, which looks good on your balance sheet and will impress future investors, and (3) with less capital there is less to lose should your new company become embroiled in a lawsuit.

Here are some ways to reduce capital needs:
(1) Lease buildings, automobiles, or even furniture.
(2) If you are a manufacturer, have your parts machined by a subcontractor.
(3) Subcontract at least a portion of your employees.

Now in order to estimate your starting capital requirements, first figure out your operating expense requirements for the first year. Table 12-1 may serve as a guide.

The data in this table are based on an assumed $1 million in sales per year. You may have to pro-rate the amounts shown in this table, i.e., use half the numbers if you shoot for only $500,000 in sales, or double the numbers for $2 million in yearly sales. Another thing I like to point out is that these figures are based on the assumption that you may want to start a manufacturing business and are somewhat on the lean side (i.e., you should be a good manager). For a whole-sale business, the capital requirements are certainly less, but so will your profit level as a percent of sales.

TABLE 12-1
FIRST YEAR OPERATING EXPENSES
Based on $1 Million Sales

	No Leases	Leased Equipment
Wages/salaries	$195,000	$195,000
Wage related overhead	57,000	57,000
Sales expenses	125,000	125,000
Advertising	10,000	10,000
Shipping expenses	20,000	20,000
Travel expenses	8,000	8,000
Telephone/fax	4,000	4,000
Insurance*	3,000	3,000
Supplies	5,000	5,000
Utilities	3,000	3,000
Legal/Accounting	5,000	5,000
Interest**	74,000	34,000
Cost of material	285,000	285,000
Rent/Lease payments	0	100,000
TOTAL	$794,000	$854,000
Profit before Tax and Depreciation: ($ 1 Mio Less Operating Expenses)	$206,000	$146,000
Return on Capital:	14%	21.5%
Profit as % of Sales:	20.6%	14.6%

---

* Could be substantially higher if product liability insurance is
  involved and you have no product history.

** Assuming a bank loan on 50% of starting capital (see Table 12-2) at
  10% interest.

As you can see, it makes a difference on whether or not you lease buildings and tool machinery. If you own buildings and machinery, the yearly expenses are less $794,000 versus $854,000 when leasing due to the added lease payments. However, if you look at the capital requirements shown in Table 12-2, you find the situation reversed. Without a lease, you need $1,475,000 and with a lease, you only need $680,000-or roughly half. Now the profit (before tax and depreciation) is $206,000 without a lease versus $146,000 with a lease. This makes a return on capital invested of 14.0% versus 21.5% before tax and makes leasing an attractive option, although you might miss the tax savings due to depreciation.

Notice that I added a 1/2-year's worth of expenses to the capital requirements. The fact that your initial sales will only start slowly and that customers typically pay their bills four to six weeks after the goods have been shipped to them, can make for a very tight cash situation at least for the first six months. This is a fact commonly overlooked by many budding entrepreneurs, who when faced by such an emergency have to go to such unpleasant means as delaying payment of salaries and taxes, or not paying their vendors. All actions fraught with great danger!

In some businesses, a reserve of half of the yearly expenses is not enough. For example, if you want to start out as a manufacturing representative in a new territory, then a year's expenses will be necessary as a safety cushion in order to keep you alive.

TABLE 12-2
REQUIRED STARTING CAPITAL
For projected sales of $1 Mio per Year

	No Leases	Leased Equipment
Cash	$10,000	$10,000
Accounts receivable	115,000	115,000
Inventory	180,000	180,000
Deposits	5,000	25,000
Land	150,000	0
Building	200,000	0
Factory machinery	450,000	0
Small tools & fixtures	50,000	50,000
Vehicles	25,000	0
Computer software	5,000	5,000
Furniture/computers	25,000	5,000
Literature	5,000	5,000
6-month operating cash flow*	255,000	285,000
TOTAL	**$1,475,000**	**$680,000**

*50% of one-year operating expenses from Table 12-1 less cost of
material (already included in inventory).

How to structure your company

Most people assume that the moment you start your own
business you have to get incorporated. This is mostly unnecessary and quite often foolish. Let's review the advantages
and disadvantages of the various options:

Proprietorship. This means you own your own business and there are no shareholders. The income passes directly to you and you report it on your IRS Form 1040, Schedule C. A big advantage is there is no paperwork hassles, franchise tax payments, and so on. The biggest disadvantage is that should you ever go bankrupt, your creditors will go after your private assets and bank accounts.

Incorporation (Inc.). Here your company becomes a separate legal entity with its own personality and rules. The corporation papers have to be filed with the secretary of state, usually in the state where you live. The corporation has to follow certain specified rules such as having to have stockholder meetings, and elected officers. Tax disadvantages are that you have to pay double taxation unless your earnings are small, i.e., your corporation pays a corporate income tax and your stockholders pay again a tax on dividends paid from the same earnings.

Some people use a corporation to accumulate value by not paying dividends (you still have to pay corporate income taxes!). Later on, you can either sell the company (pay lower capital gain taxes), or leave the company to your children; however, there are better ways of doing this (read on). The biggest advantage of a corporation is that you can sell stock in the open market in order to raise cash for growth.

Also consider this; if you are a professional, such as an

accountant or medical practitioner, your corporate umbrella does not protect you from professional liability (e.g., a malpractice suit).

A Limited Partnership (Ltd.). This means you must have at least one partner. One of you has to be the general partner, i.e., the person who runs the company and assumes all liability (limited partners in contrast are like stockholders; they are shielded from liability). This then usually requires that the general partner should be a corporation in order to provide protection to the person who owns the general partnership. Other disadvantages include limitation in the number of partners and foreign ownership restrictions. Tax advantages include no double taxation, i.e., all earnings are taxed to you as an individual. None is paid by the partnership except to some states in the form of business profit tax. Your personal tax liability for company earnings can pose a cash flow problem, and the limited partnership usually has to pay at least sufficient funds to the partners enabling them to pay this income tax. This is cash not available for growth and expansion. Another limitation is that you cannot freely sell your share of the partnership, and you are typically required to obtain the approval of the other partners.

Limited Liability Companies (LLC). This is the latest, and only recently approved, form of business ownership. It basically combines most of the advantages of a corporation and those of a limited partnership. *Hence*, a member of an LLC is shielded from liability (except criminal), and you do not need to have a general partner. There is also no limitation in the number of members. The tax treatment is exactly like a partnership. To me, this is the best way to start your business. Perhaps the only drawback is the restriction of the transfer of shares. Nevertheless, you can always change the LLC into a corporation when your company has grown big enough to need lots of capital in order for you to become another Bill Gates.

Proprietorships, Ltd.'s, and LLC's all have one inconvenience. Apparently, these types of associations are not trusted by the IRS and all your customers, purchasing more than a few hundred dollars worth of product from your company, are required to file a form 1099 at the end of the year. This imposes a burden on them and, therefore, may hamper your sales efforts. The way out is to form a separate corporation that does only the selling and invoicing for the rest of the company, which then remains an LLC or Ltd., and, thus, avoids double taxation.

Chapter 12

WHAT DO THEY MEAN WHEN THEY SAY....AN IRREVERENT GLOSSARY

"A rose by any other name is just as sweet."
— *William Shakespeare*

Not too long ago, the government started to define heretofore clearly understood words into new verbiage in order to obscure their true meaning. For example, changing the name of the former, more to the point, War Department, to Defense Department. Unfortunately, corporate America has followed suit.

While most of you may be familiar with at least some of the newly minted expressions, I thought it might be helpful to have some translations handy. They should help you understand what is truly said being said in any meeting you attend.

A

Action Item
Work assignment for committee member. Also serves to help write agenda for next meeting.

B

Bankruptcy
When there is no more money left and you are at the mercy of your creditors.

Benchmarking
A look at what your competitors are doing.

Best cost producer
Being able to purchase material from the best qualified supplier, not necessarily from the cheapest supplier.

Board of Directors
A committee that supervises the company president whose members are elected by the shareholders, but usually are selected by the president.

Budget
A yearly sales target selected by management, seldom kept if it were not for price increases and inflation.

Business ethics
See Criminal Law

C

Capital Asset
Something you buy that can be depreciated. Affects only your cash flow, not your profit.

Chief Information Officer (CIO)
Top manager for computer systems. This person is supported by a number of consultants for technical know-how.

Committee Organization
Structure in which groups of individuals jointly hold authority and responsibility (no single person can be blamed).

Computer Aided Design (CAD)
Using a mouse instead of a pencil to create a drawing.

Competing
A war between companies conducted with other means.

Cost of Quality
A misnomer. Should be: Cost of no quality.

Creative Selling
The art of being a successful salesman.

Cross-functional Team
Different departments trying to work together on a common project. A good way to create delays.

Customer satisfaction (increasing)
Being able to reduce the number of complaints about your product and service.

D

Delegation
Unpleasant work assigned to others.

Differentiation
Why my product is better than yours.

Downsizing
Laying off employees, usually those with higher salaries and more experience.

E

Empowering
Letting you decide when to go to lunch.

Enhance bottom line
Reduce cost.

Entrepreneurship
Ability that is lacking in most managers.

Enterprise System
Computer version of how a company is thought to be organized.

Environmental Technician
Janitor

E-Mail
Method of communicating via a computer keyboard instead of speaking directly to the person in the next office.

Executive Assistant
Secretary

H

Hardware
The portion of a computer system you can actually touch.

Human Resources Dept.
Personnel Department

Human Resources
Employees

I

Income Statement
Your income and expenses.

Informal Communication Channels
Gossip

Integrated Marketing Communication (IMC)
Combining all advertising

Internal Customer
An employee from a different department.

Internet
Means to connect different computers usually via telephone wires (see E-Mail)

Inventory Control
The art of balancing the purchasing of parts with the shipment of finished goods.

ISO 9000
Clever method to enrich consultants.

J
Just-in-Time (JIT)
Near perfect execution of inventory control where actual in-house inventory approaches zero.

L
Leadership
An assumed management ability.

Local Area Network (LAN)
A system that connects a number of computers in a given area.

Loss Prevention Specialist
Security guard

M
Marketing Research
An effort to collect data from customers and competitors to help launch your product. To be effective, the person promoting the product should not do it.

Macroeconomics
The study of the company's finances in view of the national economy.

Microeconomics
The study of whether or not to give you a raise.

Mission Statements
Modern form of company logos. Can be found on the back of business cards.

Morale
Mental attitude of employees which can be influenced by communication, raises, or bonuses.

N
Negative Deficit
Profit

Negative Economic Growth
Recession

Not-for-profit Organization
Tax exempt forms with unusually high advertising budgets and management salaries.

O
Order Processing
Order entry.

Order Fulfillment
The entire process from order entry to the shipment of goods.

Organization Chart
A listing of company managers and their relationship to each other.

Outsourcing
Purchasing goods from somebody else.

Ownership
Taking ownership means you have been assigned a task.

P

Parent Company
An organization that owns a subsidiary.

Performance Appraisal
A method of filling out forms to either deny or grant raises to an employee.

Portfolio Manager
Stock broker

Positive Cash Flow
Making money without paying taxes.

Price Adjustment
Price increase

Procurement
Purchasing

Product Differentiation
Convincing your customers that your products are better than those of your competitors even though the price might be higher (see creative selling).

Product Launch
Introduction of a new product to the market. Usually done before the product is ready.

Product Liability
A means to extract money from firms or insurance companies, usually based on assumed defects of products.

Production Planning
Telling the machine shop how many parts to produce, or the Purchasing Dept. how much inventory to buy.

Productivity
A means to determine profitability.

R

Re-engineering
Usually means down-sizing the company if profit is low.

Research and Development
Efforts, usually by a team of engineers, to design a new product from specifications developed by a marketing team. Success usually is inverse proportional to the number of team members.

Resume
What people write when company morale is low.

S

Sales Associate
Salesperson

Self-management Team
A group of employees on there own if their manager is absent.

Seller's Market
Where the price of goods can be set without worrying about competitors.

Service Technician
Repairman

Social Responsibility
Management's actions to combat (usually) government perceived misbehavior.

Software
Invisible instructions to tell the computer what to do. Usually written by persons unfamiliar with your business and obsolete at time of purchase.

Statistical Quality Control
A fancy name to express the average dimensional error in a machined part's dimension.

Strategic Alliance
Usually long-term purchasing agreement between a seller and a buyer based on a guaranteed price discount.

Strategic Planning
Usually a five-year sales and financial performance forecast.

Ship on Time
Shipping goods on day of promise.

SWOT Analysis
Assessment of company's strengths and weaknesses usually through the eyes of a consultant.

T

Task Specific Role
Execution of "action item" by a committee member.

Team
Group of people on a project and devoid of any personal responsibility for the task.

Team Cohesiveness
Usually enhanced by joint golf games.

Telemarketing
People telephoning you during dinner.

Territory Managers
Outside salesmen

Total Quality Management (TQM)
Public expression of management's commitment to quality of its product. Usually an action of last resort.

V

Variable Cost
Cost of labor and material usually overshadowed by fixed cost (administrative expenses).

Voice Mail
Form of communication where
you can carry on a conversation
without ever speaking directly
to the person you called.

Index